In Shakespeare's Playhouse

MACBETH

In Shakespeare's Playhouse

Other volumes are in preparation

Maurice Percival

IN SHAKESPEARE'S PLAYHOUSE

BY
RONALD WATKINS
AND
JEREMY LEMMON

MACBETH

ROWMAN AND LITTLEFIELD
Totowa, New Jersey

First published in the United States 1974
by Rowman and Littlefield, Totowa, N.J.

ISBN 0-87471-530-X

Printed and bound in Great Britain

CONTENTS

PREFATORY NOTE

In this reconstruction of Shakespeare's play we have aimed to preserve a sense of the continuity of performance. It is important that the text of the play itself should be kept constantly in mind: quotations from the episode under discussion are printed in bold; quotations from other parts of the play, and from other plays or books, have been placed inside inverted commas. In the quotations we have made as little departure from the lineation and punctuation of the early texts as has seemed compatible with the convenience of a modern reader; spelling, however, has been modernised. We have quoted stage-directions only from the Quartos and First Folio, since these, in most cases, may reasonably be supposed to reflect the practice of performance in Shakespeare's own playhouse; they are printed as they appear in the early texts, in italics, and not modernised in any way (except that we have abandoned the long 's', and the 'i' and 'u' which represent, respectively, 'j' and 'v').

For those readers who wish to keep Shakespeare's text by them as they read, we have added in the margin Act, Scene and Line numbers, as milestones of the play's progress. Since no universally standardised system of reference-numbering is yet conveniently available, we have chosen in these and other reference-numbers to follow the *Oxford Standard Authors* edition of Shakespeare's Works (edited by W. J. Craig), except when, for a particular purpose, another edition is specified.

Superior figures in the textual commentary refer to the Notes which are grouped together at the end of the book.

INTRODUCTION

In April 1611 Doctor Simon Forman saw MACBETH at the Globe Playhouse. His account is incomplete and confused, but there is no doubt
that in this description of 'Mackbeth at the Glob' we have the earliest
recorded evidence of a performance of Shakespeare's tragedy in the
public theatre. Nevertheless, although the play did not appear in print
until the publication of the First Folio edition of Shakespeare's plays
in 1623, we can be certain that it made its first appearance on the stage
some years earlier even than the performance Forman saw in 1611:
most scholars agree that it was written in 1606, and was seen in that
year at the Globe, and perhaps, in Court performance, at Greenwich
or Hampton Court; indeed, Henry N. Paul, *The Royal Play of Macbeth*,
argues that the very first performance of MACBETH was at Hampton
Court on 7 August 1606, and that it was specially written to form part
of the celebrations which marked the state visit of Christian IV of
Denmark to his brother-in-law, James I of England, in the summer of
that year. Whether or not Shakespeare conceived his play for this purpose we cannot be certain, but it does seem to reflect the known tastes
and preoccupations of the king who for so many years ruled Scotland
as James VI before he became James I of England. Warlike and valiant
Scots had appeared before in Shakespeare's plays (and an elaborate
and scabrous joke in THE COMEDY OF ERRORS involves the 'barrenness'
of Scotland, with the same hackneyed tradition of music-hall humour
as it invokes the 'bogs' of Ireland and the 'chalky Cliffs' of England);
but MACBETH is his first attempt at the serious and extensive handling
of a Scottish theme. The play seems to reflect, too, the King's pride in
his ancestry, his well-known interest in witchcraft, his views on the
nature of kingship and on the action of conscience after a man has

turned to wickedness, and his concern with the question whether imagination could produce effects which seemed to be real; and scholars have detected many other ways in which the tastes of James I seem to underlie the words and action of Shakespeare's play; it is even possible that the King's preference for short plays may have led Shakespeare to cut or compress a longer version of MACBETH.

But Shakespeare was not concerned merely to create an ephemeral entertainment for the pleasure of a royal patron: although it is true that the preoccupations of the King seem to lie at the roots of the play, again and again these preoccupations, in the hands of the poet, are made to serve the essential purposes of a drama conceived in universal terms. The episode, for instance, of the English Doctor (IV.iii.140 ff.) seems to be a topical commentary on the ceremony of the royal touch by which, so it was believed, the disease called scrofula, or the King's Evil, could be cured; James did not wholly care for the tradition he had inherited from his Tudor predecessors, but he came ultimately to see that the ritual played a not unimportant part in emphasising the 'Divinity' that 'doth hedge a King'. Yet this episode is not, as it has sometimes been considered, relevant only to Court performance: it plays its part, as we shall see, in the structure of the play, deploying images both of sickness and of holiness which are essential to Shakespeare's purpose. We shall come a little nearer to an understanding of Shakespeare's craft if we remember that he habitually conceived even his historical and classical plays in terms of his own time. Sir James Fergusson, *Shakespeare's Scotland*, 12, 21, places Shakespeare's debt to the King in perspective, when he discusses the imaginative response necessary to 'a proper appreciation of the tragedy of *Macbeth*, whether in the study or on the stage'. We must think of Shakespeare's Scotland 'not as that of a remote and practically unknown eleventh century but as that of Mary, Queen of Scots, and the Regencies, of the two turbulent Earls of Bothwell, of Stirling and Kirk o'Field and Gowrie House. . . . It is the Scotland of King James VI that was Shakespeare's Scotland.'

MACBETH was written at a momentous time. The discovery of the Gunpowder Plot in November 1605 created in London an atmosphere of terror which lasted for several months. It is likely that Shakespeare knew some of the conspirators personally, and even if we do not accept the suggestion that MACBETH was designed for Court performance, it is not surprising that it should bear the mark of 'dire Combustion, and confus'd Events, New hatch'd to th' woeful time'. It is not the first time that Shakespeare has been concerned with regicide, and with the disorder of a divided realm, but to an audience of 1606 the story of a good king delivered from treason and rebellion only to be assassinated by a secret traitor must have held a special significance. Once again, we may see how the concerns of the day were transmuted to serve the interests of Shakespeare's play. The fine description of Cawdor's death (I.iv.2 ff.) may be related to the career of Sir Everard Digby, an attractive and popular figure in whom James I had taken a personal interest; he became implicated in the Plot and died deeply penitent for his treason. This passage is a powerful instrument, not only in conveying the nature of the sainted King Duncan, but also in establishing Shakespeare's theme of the false face hiding the treacherous heart. This theme finds expression later (I.v.66 f.) in a striking image: 'look like th'innocent flower, But be the Serpent under't.' After the discovery of the Plot a medal had been struck, bearing the device of a serpent concealed among flowers. In other ways, too, Shakespeare draws upon the circumstances of the Plot in his handling of the theme, pervasive in the play, of deceitfulness, subtle or flagrant, of one who 'swears, and lies', of the fine distinction between direct untruth and the truth itself used for deception. The doctrine of Equivocation, for instance, came into prominence at the trial, in March 1606, of the Jesuit Henry Garnet, accused of complicity in the Plot. Garnet claimed that a man could be justified for lying under oath, provided that he did so for the sake of his faith and with mental reservations; this was not perjury but equivocation. Garnet was executed in May, and on the scaffold he confessed that 'It is no time now to equivocate'. The people of London, patriotic and Protestant, would have agreed with the Porter in consigning to Hell the Equivocator 'who committed Treason enough for God's sake, yet could not equivocate to Heaven'; and an imaginative sympathy with their feelings will help us to appreciate the horror with which Macbeth describes the subtlest kind of deception, 'th'Equivocation of the Fiend, That lies like truth'. Lenox's description of the storm which is among the unnatural portents accompanying Duncan's murder perhaps reflects the fearful hurricane which devastated England, as if in divine or diabolic comment, on the day after Garnet's conviction: the forces of nature themselves are turbulent when there is unnatural treason in the state.

The most significant implication arising out of the date of MACBETH, however, is its position in Shakespeare's career as a playwright: it follows hard upon OTHELLO and KING LEAR, and immediately precedes ANTONY AND CLEOPATRA and CORIOLANUS: when he wrote this play, Shakespeare's tragic inspiration was at its climax of intensity. Yet it has not always received whole-hearted admiration. The most outspoken of modern critics is G. B. Harrison (*Shakespeare's Tragedies*), who argues that, although MACBETH contains 'excellencies which Shakespeare nowhere else surpassed', it is a play 'so full of blemishes that it is hard to believe one man wrote it'. He sees signs of collaboration, interpolation or revision; he sees also much 'hasty writing'. And all this is, he suggests, the result of the play's genesis: it is 'a play hurriedly put together for a royal performance'. This kind of criticism cannot be wholly ignored; indeed, to the careful reader, turning over the pages of a printed text at his leisure, some of it seems uncomfortably well-aimed. But in the theatre, even the proscenium theatre, a different picture emerges; and if we could see MACBETH performed in the kind of theatre for which Shakespeare wrote, the picture would be clearer still. The aim of this volume, as of the other volumes in this series, is to reconstruct in imagination a performance of Shakespeare's play in his own lifetime, and thereby to throw the clearest possible light upon its overall design and the minute detail of its writing. The principles upon which our attempted reconstruction proceeds are set forth in our Introductory Volume, but we append here a brief recapitulation to prepare the reader for a visit to THE TRAGEDIE OF MACBETH as presented at the Globe playhouse in the daylight of a London afternoon in the year 1606. We ask him to bear in mind certain known facts about the circumstances of Shakespeare's working life, and some conclusions which may be drawn from them:

(1) During most of the period when he was writing his plays, Shakespeare was an active member of the most successful players' company in London; certainly at the time of the performance of MACBETH which we seek to reconstruct, he was present at, and presumably taking a personal part in, the preparation and rehearsal of his plays.

(2) The plays were written to be performed by the regular members of the company—the body which had recently received the royal patronage of James I and was known, therefore, as the King's Men. It has been said of Shakespeare's creative method that 'the play was regularly fitted to the company, not the company to the play' and that his plays 'represent not only his own individual invention but also the collective invention of his company' (T. W. Baldwin, *The Organization and Personnel of the Shakespearean Company*, 197, 303). Shakespeare's conception, not only of the role of Macbeth with its huge imaginative range, but also of the minor characters (the 'cream-fac'd Loon', the dry-tongued Scottish Doctor, the benevolent Old Man), sprang partly from the appearance and personality of the players at his disposal.

(3) The plays were presented in repertory—six different plays, by various authors, in a week—repeated at intervals only as long as they were successful in drawing an audience. These conditions preclude the idea of a director's designing and dressing a play as for a long run. Whatever may have been the special resources of costume and stage-furniture by which the company brought Macbeth's Scotland into the playhouse in visible terms, they were not the chief means of conveying the world of the play to the audience.

(4) The company was extremely adaptable in performance; it was accustomed to appear at court or on tour, as well as in its own playhouse. We do not know for certain whether MACBETH was consciously written for performance at Hampton Court, or whether it appeared first at the Globe; but we can be tolerably sure that the company was ready to perform the play in both places—and in others too. Nevertheless, their home in 1606 was the Globe, and at that period of Shakespeare's career his plays were for the most part conceived for this milieu, the daily setting of his working life; we

may assume that the physical and atmospheric conditions of performance in the public playhouse were constantly in his mind as he composed.

(5) Shakespeare's Globe was octagonal, polygonal or circular, small but capacious, and open to the skies. We do not know its precise dimensions, but we may guess that the overall diameter was less than 100 feet, possibly as little as 80 feet; and that the diameter of the interior (with which we are chiefly concerned) was considerably less than the 78 feet which is the length of a lawn-tennis court. Yet its capacity was more than 2,000. The performance therefore could touch the extremes of intimacy and public address; each individual hearer, even in the Galleries, was the personal confidant of Macbeth in his anguished wrestling with his motives, and an eavesdropper upon the exchange of panic-stricken whispers after the murder of Duncan. By contrast, Duncan's address, early in the play, to 'Sons, Kinsmen, Thanes', and Malcolm's, at the end, to 'My Thanes and Kinsmen', are public and ceremonial in tone, involving in a moment of ritual the spectators in the crowded playhouse no less than the players on the Stage. The transition from one mode of address to another could be rapid: Macbeth turns instantly from private conversation with Banquo to an address to his court: 'Let every man be master of his time. . . .' (III.i.41).

(6) The great Stage projected into the audience, which sat or stood on three sides of it. The middle of the front of the Stage was the central point of the whole building. The background of the Stage was formed by the façade of the Tiring-House, behind which the actors attired themselves: in it were set two Doors, one on either side, through which the actors emerged on to the Stage. For much of the time the Stage was treated as independent of this background, as, for instance, during the second scene of the play: the bare Stage does not represent the precise locality favoured by editors ('The King's Camp' or 'Forres'); instead, with the help of physical circumstance (the sound of alarums, the sight of the bleeding Captain the mime of the actors), and above all of the poet's word, we are free to watch in the mind's eye battle and rebellion as they unfold before us. Sometimes we are made acutely aware of an unseen

geography behind the Tiring-House: while, in I.vii, Macbeth hesitates, we know that, just out of sight, his royal guest is feasting in the Great Hall; more striking still is our awareness, during the long sequence of the murder, of the proximity of Duncan's bedchamber. And sometimes, as in the scene between Rosse and the Old Man, the Stage represents no locality at all.

(7) The Tiring-House, though the details of its architecture are uncertain, was a permanent feature of the playhouse, familiar and accepted by the audience every time they came to the play. It could therefore be ignored altogether or, if such was the dramatist's wish, its features could be used, described and embodied in the action. While the Stage represents a heath, we do not see the Door by which Macbeth and Banquo enter to meet the Witches—the physical eye is directed by the imagination. But at the poet's wish the Tiring-House façade becomes the castle of Inverness, about which the martlets fly; and at the end of the play it becomes the stronghold of Dunsinane, and we see it clearly when Siward invites Malcolm to 'Enter Sir, the Castle'.

(8) Because of the proportions of Stage and auditorium, by which an actor could stand at the very central point of the whole playhouse, the audience were not detached spectators of a remote picture but engaged participants, often partisans, on the fringe of a live action taking place in their midst. This truth emerges particularly in scenes of crowd and battle; it emerges too in those cases where the playwright asks us to watch a play within his play: in MACBETH, when the curtains of the discovery-space open at the Witches' command to reveal *A shew of eight Kings*, there is little barrier of division between the watching Macbeth and the audience in the playhouse: he, like us, is a spectator for a moment at a 'show'.

(9) This relationship was emphasised by the fact that the performance took place in the neutral daylight of a London afternoon, the audience and the players being in the same light. Elaborate lighting effects and the deliberate directing of light were impossible: atmosphere, therefore, and subtleties of characterisation and shifting moods were created by other means—the gestures and miming of the actors, and the spoken word, often conveying to the mind's eye

what the physical eye could not see. In MACBETH Shakespeare called upon the highest resources of his art to bring darkness into the daylit theatre; and only a detailed analysis in the sequence of performance can demonstrate the skill of the gradual process by which he achieved his purpose—beginning with the 'fog and filthy air' of the Witches, continuing through the invocations of Macbeth ('Stars hide your fires') and his Wife ('Come thick Night'), and through the *Torches* of Duncan's arrival, until the starless night settles into the playhouse, and becomes in its turn unnatural darkness which even the morning sun cannot dissipate. And several times later in the play, too, darkness is again invoked, most notably (by a poetic spell of unsurpassed power) just before the 'dark hour' of Banquo's murder.

(10) The female parts were played by boy-actors, and the illusion of femininity was created by the same means—the words of the dramatist and the intonations, gestures and miming of the players (not only those who played the female parts but also those who acted with them and spoke to and about them). If we bear this truth in mind, we shall look with new eyes at the role of Lady Macbeth, distant as it is from the ingenuous heroines of Shakespeare's early plays. Yet, while the emotional range is greater, the boy's most effective weapon is still the spoken word. And it is with the confidence of assured success that the poet can make his boy-player demand (as Lady Macbeth invokes the power of evil which is to possess her) 'unsex me here' and 'Come to my Woman's Breasts': it is a challenge to the disbelief of the audience.

Now since, in the absence of precise evidence, our reconstruction involves prudent conjecture, we ask the reader to accept as a setting for all that follows the architectural features of the drawing which appears as our frontispiece. The great *Stage* is the main acting arena. The *Doors* are the chief means of access to the Stage from the Tiring-House; they are tall and broad enough to accommodate Malcolm's army carrying the leafy boughs of Birnam Wood. Between the Doors is the discovery-space which (for convenience of reference, and without any associative intention) we shall call the *Study*; its chief use is simply as an extension of the Stage, since the revealing of properties or furniture (like the throne where Lady Macbeth 'keeps her State' in III.iv) may suggest locality or character for the whole Stage; but when the hangings of the Study part to reveal the *shew of eight Kings*, the Study becomes a miniature theatre in its own right. There is, too, an inset space on the upper level which we shall call the *Chamber*. Set well forward on the Stage are the two *Stage-Posts*; the poet is not averse to using them for the purposes of atmosphere or action, but in common with the other minor structural features they are for the most part ignored; they do, however, serve to give shape and pattern to the bare Stage—we shall see how the sense of distance is created on the broad and deep Stage when the Witches wait menacingly outside one Post, close to the groundlings, while Macbeth makes his first appearance at the far Door (I.iii). The structural purpose of the Posts is to support the *Heavens*, the painted canopy (overhanging the Stage and protecting the players from inclement weather) which gives visible substance to Rosse's image of the disordered universe: 'Thou seest the Heavens, as troubled with man's Act, Threatens his bloody Stage. . . .' The *Trap-Door* in the centre of the Stage is used for certain conjuring-tricks (the appearance of Banquo's Ghost, the descent of the cauldron), but it is also part of the emblematic cosmology of the playhouse suggested in Rosse's lines; for beneath it is *Hell*, from which, with peculiar propriety, the three Apparitions rise in thunder at the Witches' commands. Here then, lying between the Heavens and Hell, Shakespeare's Stage is all this world, the physical setting for which he conceived Macbeth's phrases of despair:

Life's but a walking Shadow, a poor Player,
That struts and frets his hour upon the Stage . . .

Above the Heavens are the *Huts*, from which trumpet and banner summon us to the play, and from which thunder sounds; it is, indeed, the play's first sound, and it will combine with the poet's word to bring the violence of the disturbed elements into the daylit playhouse.

Inevitably, since the structural features of the playhouse are themselves partly conjectural, the precise use made of them by Shakespeare's company is very much matter for debate. And we must never forget that he and his fellows were often obliged to perform in conditions (at court or on tour) which were very different in structural detail from those of the public playhouse: even the Trap-Door which accommodates the cauldron as it 'sinks' cannot always have been available. The swift continuity of Shakespeare's plays, their insistent dramatic relevance, does indeed seem to reflect some distribution of scenes between the different acting areas of Stage and Tiring-House, but it is a fruitless quest to seek for systematic formulas of scene-rotation: each play, we submit, called upon the resources of the playhouse in its own way. The last Act of MACBETH is often, in performance today, an anticlimax: the strong and economical development of the first part of the play is succeeded, it seems, by a clumsy and confused narrative of invasion and battle, interspersed, but not integrated, with a few powerful moments of personal tragedy. We shall see how the geography of the playhouse serves to clarify the action of this last Act; and not only that—we shall see, too, how the emotional and dramatic effect of Shakespeare's conception is so compellingly conveyed that the structure of the playhouse seems to reflect the structure of the play itself.

We shall bear in mind, then, all the features we have described as we trace the course of the action of MACBETH: but while it is easy to over-emphasise the importance of the part played by the minor structural features of the playhouse in the development of Shakespeare's craft, we must never forget that the greater part of the action took place on the bare Stage, and that comparatively little use was made of the other features we have mentioned. Meanwhile, we may isolate three conditions of performance in Shakespeare's theatre which were immutable; and these are of cardinal importance in seeking a full appreciation of his dramatic skills:

(A) a stage or acting area which projected from its background, and on which the action was three-dimensional, like sculpture, not two-dimensional, like painting; so that the audience was closely involved in the action;

(B) a background which was permanent and unchanging, always basically the same (with perhaps different hangings for tragedy, comedy or history, and other adjusted features of furniture or properties to suit the play of the afternoon) and architecturally constant. The audience, entering the playhouse, knew what they would see, and could ignore the features of the background, if the dramatist so wished. The excited interest, at the first performance of each new play, would be—what will they turn it into this time?

(C) a constant and neutral light, embracing players and audience alike, so that the illusion of light and darkness, or weather or atmosphere, or subtle characterisation, must be created by the miming, gesture and posture of the actors, and above all by the words which the playwright gave them to speak.

*   *   *

The earliest printed text of MACBETH appeared in the First Folio edition of Shakespeare's plays in 1623; it is this text, therefore, that we use as our prompt-book, as we seek to reconstruct a performance of THE TRAGEDIE OF MACBETH at the Globe in 1606. Since there are no earlier editions with which to compare the Folio text, the task of editors and commentators is in one sense simplified; paradoxically, however, the very absence of comparable texts opens the door for all manner of editorial speculations and conjecture, and the Folio text (printed, it seems likely, from a playhouse prompt-book) has often been attacked as untrustworthy. MACBETH is remarkably short in comparison with the average length of Shakespeare's plays; it is only two-thirds as long as KING LEAR. It may be that the Folio has preserved for us a cut version (cut, perhaps, in deference to James I's taste for short plays). There are loose threads, both of plot and character, such as might be due to the compression of a longer version. Although, for instance, the Folio directs that Macduff should arrive at Inverness with the King's retinue in I.vi, he does not speak until II.iii—when he is admitted to the castle by the Porter after Duncan's murder; and he is not identified by name for the audience until much later in that scene. It is possible that in this oblique and belated introduction of an important character there is evidence of an excision. It has been suggested that Lady Macbeth's reference to an occasion when her husband first proposed 'this enterprise' to her (I.vii.48) implies the existence of a scene not preserved in the Folio; it has even been suggested that, since certain details in Forman's account of the performance he saw in 1611 do not match Shakespeare's play (in his confused memory Forman has blended Shakespeare's version of the story with Holinshed's), they may be treated as further evidence of lost scenes. The most celebrated inconsistency appears in Macbeth's incredulous line, in reception of the Witch's greeting, 'The Thane of Cawdor lives A prosperous Gentleman.' In the previous scene it has been made clear to us that Macbeth does indeed know of Cawdor's treason and defeat. But inconsistency of detail is a not uncommon feature of Shakespeare's writing: himself a practising man of the theatre, he knew well enough what was important, and what was not, for the practical purpose of casting a spell over the audience. So compelling and insistent is the narrative relevance of the play as a whole, and so strong are the ironies conveyed in the unbroken continuity of carefully juxtaposed scenes, that, if it is a cut version of a longer original, the cutting was probably done by, or with the agreement of, the poet himself.

Critics have also claimed, on stylistic grounds, to find in the Folio text evidence of interpolation or collaboration; but few of their charges (as, for instance, that the first scene of the Witches, the speeches of the bleeding Captain, the episode of the Porter, are all spurious) stand up to examination, and most modern scholars reject them: Harrison is an exception. Detailed analysis of the play in action (in the conditions for which it was conceived) will bring us closer to an understanding of the practical, dramatic or stylistic purpose of such passages. But not all these charges can be easily shrugged off: in two passages certainly (III.iv; IV.i.39–43) and in a third probably (IV.i.124–32) the Folio offers us interpolations by a hand other than Shakespeare's. There is insufficient space here to deal fully with the grounds for regarding the Hecate episodes as spurious; the interested reader is recommended to turn to Kenneth Muir's summary in his *Arden* edition of the play (xxxv ff.). Most editors have rejected the authenticity of these scenes for various reasons, stylistic, narrative, psychological, practical and dramatic: in particular, the stage-directions demand that the Witches should sing two songs which appear in full in Thomas Middleton's *The Witch* (they are strikingly unsuitable to Shakespeare's play); *The Witch* contains strong verbal echoes of MACBETH; and Middleton is known to have worked for the King's Men. These considerations have led editors to the conclusion that the interpolations are the work of Middleton, but Muir argues that Shakespeare's Hecate is quite unlike Middleton's, and suggests that these passages were written by 'an anonymous writer, not without poetic ability, who was instructed to explain and introduce the two songs and the dance which had been interpolated from *The Witch*'. The third suspect passage (IV.i. 124–132) does not involve Hecate, but in its tone it is of a piece with the others, and like them demands *Musicke*.[1] It is probable that these three passages were later additions, calculated to please the growing taste for theatrical spectacle, music and dancing. For this reason we do not include them in our reconstruction of MACBETH at the Globe, although we cannot assume that Shakespeare disapproved of the additions when they were finally made: his theatrical taste was probably rather less fastidious than that of his admiring critics, and he was an entertainer before he was a philosopher or a theologian. The only other serious reflection on the integrity of the Folio version arises, at least partly, out of the assumption that the first Hecate-scene is spurious: since an analysis of this charge involves a discussion in some detail of the play's action at that point, it is better postponed until we come to consider the suspect scene itself.*

With a few reservations, then, the Folio text is our prompt-book. In quotation, we reproduce, as far as possible without obscuring the sense, its punctuation and capital letters. The Folio punctuation cannot with certainty be said to be the poet's own, and several different hands (not least those of the editors, Shakespeare's fellow-players Heminges and Condell) were no doubt concerned in its distribution; yet its purpose seems in many cases to be rhetorical rather than syntactical, preserving the fluency and variety of spoken language, and it is our nearest approach to the diction of the players and the poet's phrasing. The Folio's capitals, though they cannot be analysed to represent a system of emphasis, seem nevertheless to reflect from time to time a sense of thematic proportion. We have for the most part adopted the Folio lineation too, although in this matter once again many editors

* See *page 111, below.*

have felt it to be untrustworthy: we must bear in mind the persuasive argument of Richard Flatter (*Shakespeare's Producing Hand*, 94) that the Folio text of MACBETH 'shows no traces of "editorial" interference', and that this is 'probably the only play from which the real yard-stick of Shakespeare's diction can be obtained'; the discontent of later editors he ascribes to their own misguided 'poetical demand, i.e. the demand of continuity of versification'. While it is true that the curiosities of lineation in the early texts are sometimes caused by the incompetence of the printers or the problems of type-setting by formes, they may also sometimes represent the subtlety and variety with which Shakespeare manipulates the iambic pentameter, the norm of his verse-writing. One instance must suffice: the Folio version of II.i.12–17 runs as follows:

> What Sir, not yet at rest? the King's a bed.
> He hath beene in unusuall Pleasure,
> And sent forth great Largesse to your Offices.
> This Diamond he greetes your Wife withall,
> By the name of most kind Hostesse,
> And shut up in measurelesse content.

A typical modern edition prints it thus:

> What, sir, not yet at rest? The King's abed:
> He hath been in unusual pleasure, and
> Sent forth great largess to your offices:
> This diamond he greets your wife withal,
> By the name of most kind hostess; and shut up
> In measureless content.

The moment's telling pause at the end of the second line is lost. The Folio's third line makes a natural elision of 'to your', and distributes the emphasis where it is wanted: in the modern text the word 'to' has more weight than it can conveniently bear. The penultimate line in the modern text has become hurried and clumsy. The Folio lineation suggests that the last two lines of the speech must be spoken very slowly; the words 'most kind' and 'shut up' are the most leisurely of all, each word occupying the space of a whole iambic foot. Thus the lines each contain the normal five stresses, and the atmosphere of drowsy contentment is emphasised.

While we have, for the reader's convenience, made occasional changes in the detail of the Folio text, and indeed modernised the spelling throughout, we strongly urge interpreters of Shakespeare, player and student alike, to work from the early printed texts: the quiddities of the Elizabethan and Jacobean printing-houses are no great obstacle to the judicious reader, and under the seemingly eccentric variations of spelling, punctuation, lineation, speech-headings, stage-directions, there lie many clues and trails for the detective who would unravel the mystery of what really happened on the stage of Shakespeare's Globe.

*   *   *

Those who adopt the time-honoured view that we know very little about Shakespeare's life, seem to forget that nearly twenty years of it were spent in the whole-time occupation of the playhouse—not only the penning of plays, but rehearsal, training, discussion, adjustment, explanation, improvisation, experiment; and all this among a company of colleagues who were unique in the long endurance and for the most part amicable relationship of their association. Since the range of our speculation covers not only the afternoons of performance but also the mornings of rehearsal, and even the late-night post-mortems at the Mermaid Tavern, it is part of our brief to become acquainted with Shakespeare's fellow-actors, and to let their names grow familiar in the mouth as household words. For this purpose we step still further into the field of conjecture, seeking the aid of Professor Baldwin's book which, besides expounding the facts of the company's organisation, is bold enough to dally with surmise as to the casting of roles. Though we may disagree with this or that ascription, the attempt is valuable, because it keeps us in mind of the fact that the members of the Shakespearian company provided among them the first interpreters of these acting roles which are usually discussed as if they existed in abstract independence. The part of Macbeth is played by Richard Burbage, the leading tragedian of the company: his art has developed hand in hand with Shakespeare's, and the poet can now demand from him a greater emotional range than when he created the role of Romeo. In particular, Shakespeare calls upon him to convey to the audience that subtle disparity, explored in the earlier portrait of the introspective Brutus, between the image a man holds of himself and the deeper motives and feelings that may sometimes belie it. Burbage is nearing forty; he has already played Lear, and Othello (who is 'declin'd Into the vale of years'); he was to die in 1619; it is with more than figurative pathos that Macbeth finds that his 'way of life Is fall'n into the Sere, the yellow Leaf'. Baldwin suggests that Lowin played Banquo: he is a strong and versatile actor—he has been Claudius and Iago, and he will be Enobarbus: he can keep the audience guessing as to the real nature of the equivocal Banquo. Sly has gained in stature: his line of young gallants (Laertes, Fenton, Claudio in MEASURE FOR MEASURE) has already achieved a new dimension in the villainous glamour of Edmund; now he once more crosses swords with Burbage, as Macduff. Robert Armin, the clown of the company, must of course retire into the background; and yet we shall come to a better understanding of what Coleridge called the 'disgusting passage of the Porter' if we remember that it was not written for the broad genius of Kemp, Armin's predecessor: it is a carefully observed portrait, rich in verbal implication, and finely integrated into the tragic structure of the play; Armin has been, we remember, the Fool to Burbage's Lear. The rising star among the boy-players is John Edmans; he was Regan ('Then let them Anatomise Regan: See what breeds about her heart. Is there any cause in Nature that makes these hard-hearts?'), and so well will he portray Lady Macbeth that the poet will think it worth while to invest Plutarch's Cleopatra with theatrical flesh and bones. Perhaps the poet himself takes part, as King Duncan; if the tradition is true that he played Adam in AS YOU LIKE IT, he was well fitted to communicate in the playhouse that sweetness of nature he wrote into the character of the sainted king. By keeping the presence and influence of the individual players constantly in mind, we have a vivid impression of the poet himself, ready no doubt to listen to suggestion but, because of his standing as a share-holder in the company, and his unique value as a box-office draw, allowed (is it rash to assume?) to have the last word in decision. It is with such a purpose of evoking the atmosphere of Shakespeare's 'workshop' that we print Baldwin's cast-list, conjectural though it is, for MACBETH:

Macbeth	Burbage
Banquo	Lowin
Malcolm	Condell
Rosse	Heminges
Macduff	Sly
Duncan	Shakespeare
Porter	Armin
Old Man	Cowley
Lenox	Cooke
Lady Macbeth	Edmans
Lady Macduff	Sands
Son	Robinson

*   *   *

When we come to consider what the members of Shakespeare's company looked like when they appeared on the Stage of the Globe, we must bear in mind the conditions of a weekly repertory of six plays, and discard all notions of an elaborate comprehensive design for production. Nevertheless we know that surprisingly large sums were spent on the dressing of Kings and Queens in the theatre of the time, and apart from the purchases which figure in the playhouse accounts, we are told that the nobles at court gave their discarded but still splendid garments to the players. The dresses in MACBETH would certainly be sumptuous, as befits a royal play. Moreover Shakespeare, with his sharp eye for visual effect, well knew how costumes, on the bare Stage of the Globe, could be made to serve his dramatic purpose: the sleep-walking of Lady Macbeth with, as her Gentlewoman tells us, her 'Night-Gown' thrown upon her, not only makes a memorable picture in its own right—it also recalls for us that earlier occasion when she appeared in her night-gown, hastily donned; the Folio direction *Enter Macbeth as King* indicates a change of costume which makes visible to our eyes his attainment of sovereignty; on several occasions—when Macduff in his grief pulls his hat upon his brows, when Macbeth in his fury snatches at his armour, when half-naked sleepers fill the Stage at the discovery of the murder—the poet uses details of costume to powerful dramatic effect. Of the exact nature of the costumes, we cannot, however, be certain. The play demands that some distinction be visibly made between the Scots and the English, particularly towards the end, when such a distinction is important to the playwright's conception; when Rosse appears at the English court, Malcolm recognises him as 'My Countryman' before he speaks. The costume of a Scottish soldier, clearly differentiated from the soldiers of other nations, may be seen in an illustration from Caspar Rutz, *Habitus Variarum Orbis Gentium*, 1581 (reproduced in *Shakespeare's England*, vol. 2, 116). However, although MACBETH is, in a sense, a history play, we must never forget that Shakespeare's vision of the circumstances of his story was habitually related to his own times. His references to cannons, clocks, dollars, do not strike the audience in the playhouse as anachronistic solecisms; and the references to dress, and the imagery arising out of it, suggest—when they suggest any period at all—this same contemporary view: the Porter finds matter for an obscure joke in French hose; the image of Duncan's 'Silver skin, lac'd with his Golden Blood' is derived from the spectacular dress of a Jacobean courtier, cloth of silver interlaced with gold. Incidental support for this argument may be found in the chief source-book for MACBETH, Holinshed's *Chronicles*, the vigorous illustrations of which demonstrate, like Shakespeare's play, a vision of history related to the writer's own time. We may imagine Burbage's Macbeth, then, as looking more like a Darnley or a Bothwell than an eleventh-century barbarian wearing the accoutrements (leather cross-garters and goatskins) demanded by the conventions of the realistic theatre. By the same token, Edmans's Lady Macbeth will be a great Elizabethan or Jacobean Lady.

A famous illustration in Holinshed may give us a clue to the visible guise of the Witches as Shakespeare imagined them, menacing figures dressed not in tatters, but in the conventional farthingales of the period. Shakespeare's treatment of the Witches differs in some important respects from Holinshed's account; and Banquo's description of them, 'so wild in their attire', does not perfectly match Holinshed's neatly dressed ladies; nevertheless we can be sure that the appearance of Shakespeare's Witches would have been unpleasantly familiar to his audience—not least to James I, who had himself written a treatise on witchcraft and made a practice of investigating personally (and with great enjoyment) cases of suspected witchcraft and possession. And it will be a valuable corrective to the more whimsical flights of the designer's imagination if we take Holinshed's illustration as our starting-point when we construct our imaginative picture of the Witches on the stage of the Globe.

*   *   *

While the players are occupied on the Stage, there is activity in the Tiring-House, under the Stage and in the Huts above the Heavens; for MACBETH, even without the machinery and music of the Hecate passages, makes some significant demands of a technical kind upon the company. The furniture and properties of the play—whether discovered in Study or Chamber, or carried out during the course of the action—are of the simplest kind. Some of them are prescribed in stage-directions, some can be deduced from the dialogue; they are functional or evocative; sometimes they give visible substance to the poet's word. *Dishes and Service* swiftly evoke the banquet (I.vii) where Duncan is feasted out of sight of the audience. In a later banquet (III. v), a 'state', or throne, isolates Lady Macbeth from her guests, and the table serves to conceal the first appearance of Banquo's Ghost; and we shall see with what skill the poet directs our attention to the eating-arrangements at the banquet, to prepare for that moment when the Ghost *sits in Macbeths place*: this manoeuvre suggests, a little later, the expression of Macbeth's horror, 'now they rise again . . . And push us from our stools'. More than once *Torches* combine with the poet's word to evoke darkness in the afternoon light of the playhouse, and the sudden extinguishing of one of them helps us to see, with the eye of the imagination, the confused darkness in which Banquo dies and his son escapes. The cauldron, the glassy globe, the boughs (freshly cut) of Birnam Wood, the banners hung upon the 'outward walls' of the Tiring-House, all serve to give visible reinforcement to

29

the poet's dramatic conception. At the beginning of the play the graphic narrative of the Captain tells us how Macbeth defeated the traitor Macdonwald and 'fix'd his Head upon our Battlements'; at the end of the play, the irony of Macbeth's own death is conveyed in the visual symbol of 'th'Usurper's cursed head', a stage-property familiar and hideous in its implications to all those members of Shakespeare's audience who had walked across London Bridge. And, more than once, blood (real blood, from the butcher's—the King's Men were not squeamish) brings to our eyes in physical substance one of the play's most pervasive images.

Perhaps more significant still is the contribution made, from within the Tiring-House and above the Heavens, to the sound-track of the play. Thunder from the Huts is the first sound we hear; and on several occasions this sound and the words of the players suggest that turbulence of the elements which reflects Macbeth's violation of the moral order. The familiar and evocative noise of *Alarums* which firmly places the action in the context of battle, the little clinking bell ('One Two: Why then 'tis time to do't'), the tolling alarum-bell, the cry of an owl ('Hark, peace: it was the Owl that shriek'd'), the clopping of hooves ('Hark, I hear Horses'), the *Cry within of Women*—all these play their part in unfolding the action, and in creating atmosphere. During the long sequence of Duncan's murder the poet's words repeatedly dwell upon the act of listening and the sensation of hearing and lead us to one of his most telling climaxes, the *Knocke within* which heralds the arrival of Macduff. The musicians are active too. They provide the *Drum within* which, maliciously parodied in the rhythmic incantation of the Witches, accompanies the first appearance of Macbeth; they provide too those other drums which during the last Act of the play heighten our anticipation of the final clash of armies. We hear trumpets, with their habitual associations of ceremony and battle: particularly splendid is the *Senit sounded* which combines with sumptuous dresses and the processional entry of *Lords, and Attendants* to suggest the new sovereignty of Macbeth. At the end of the play the trumpets give us not only the melancholy cadence of a *Retreat* but also the three triumphant flourishes which mark first the victory of Malcolm, then the ritual salutation of his Thanes, and finally the announcement of his coronation (and the end of the play). By way of contrast we hear too the sound of wind instruments, the *Hoboyes* which add to the serenity of Duncan's arrival at Inverness, and later suggest the ceremonious carousal of his banquet; the same sound is used as an eerie accompaniment to the *shew of eight Kings*.

* * *

But in the end, the substance of this play, as of all Shakespeare's plays, is the spoken word of his actors. We need to be constantly reminded that this is almost the whole of his legacy; and, because the conditions of his theatre needed the poetic drama, the legacy is almost complete: as the starting-point of our reconstruction, we need desire no more. That MACBETH contains, in Harrison's phrase, 'patches of incomparable poetry', there can be no dispute; but if we try to envisage the play in the conditions for which Shakespeare wrote it, we shall be seeking to understand the purpose of those other aspects of his writing which have sometimes come under attack—the inflated diction of the Captain, the doggerel tetrameters of the Witches, the tortuous and violent language of some of Macbeth's speeches, the occasional use of strained or fantastic imagery, of aphoristic phrases, of rhyming couplets, of playing upon the sound and sense of words in quibble or pun. The art of Shakespeare and his fellows involved the manipulation of the sense, shape and sounds of words, the communication of subtle and varied rhythms, as well as more conventional skills: the handling of soliloquy and speaking *aside* (particularly important in this play, where the public utterance of the speakers so often belies their thoughts), the representation of character in speech, the use of rhetoric to persuade or convince. And it must be supposed that the crown of their accomplishment, the skill in which they were most rigorously and successfully trained, was the ability to convey to the mind's eye of their audience all the pictures conjured up in Shakespeare's text; for of all poets he is the most pictorial. These pictures may take the form of narrative, as when Malcolm tells us of the penitent death of Cawdor; they may take the form of character-sketching, or the description of a momentary mood; or the creation of atmosphere; the description of a picture we do not see, or the interpretative recalling of a picture we have already seen; or figurative imagery, an extended image or a thumb-nail sketch to illustrate a point—like Lady Macbeth's evocation of Hope, green and pale after a night's carousal. Sometimes a pervasive image may have a powerful influence on the play's dramatic effect. Only by tracing each sequence in the context of Shakespeare's play-house can we recognise the completeness of Shakespeare's play; more-over this analysis must be made not by arbitrary thematic selection, but in the sequence of the play itself as we see it in performance. We do not imply that the many literary studies of the play, with their different purposes (psychological, philosophical, theological) are unfruitful: but our purpose is a different one—an examination of the playwright's craft in action, with an implicit belief that he knew (as so many of his interpreters, on the stage and in the study, seem unwilling to admit) how to make a play. Even when our interpretation is open to debate, we hope there is matter enough in this reconstruction to demonstrate the truth of our belief that there is no need to 'improve' upon Shakes-peare's work. Seeing MACBETH in Shakespeare's playhouse, we can understand the paradox that the dramatic unity of the play is con-veyed by an astonishing variety of skills, and that in this most eco-nomical of his tragedies the playwright's poetic and verbal invention is at its most opulent.

The Tragedy
of
MACBETH

[I.i.1-12]   The story of Macbeth ends on the battle-field. It begins likewise with a battle, but the well-known sounds of *Alarum within*, the sounds which Shakespeare's audience were used to hearing as a token of military engagement, are not the first that we hear; they emerge from a confusion of sound-effects from the Huts above the Heavens and the upper level of the Tiring-House. *Thunder and Lightning. Enter three Witches.* The noise of storm, the cries of the familiar spirits that attend upon the Witches, above all the dialogue of the Witches themselves invest the battle of the play's opening with a greater and more fateful significance than the simple issue of military victory and defeat.

The prelude takes place in mid-air, and it seems likely therefore that the Witches are disclosed on the upper level, as they **Hover** and are ready to part (in three different directions) **through the fog and filthy air**. In their position aloft they will, at the opening of the play, be detached, without a local habitation, brooding over the Stage which is to be the province of their malign influence. They have met in order to make a plan. When their plan becomes action, they will join the world of human beings and we shall see them at close quarters (on the main Stage) for the first time just before their meeting with Macbeth. In this way the structure of the playhouse gives point to the structure of the narrative.

The Witches begin by contributing in words to the storm which is already raging in sound; but that the battle, which is still undecided, is Shakespeare's initial point of emphasis, we learn in the reply to the first Witch's opening question:

When the Hurly-burly's done,
When the Battle's lost, and won.

And we are led, by a favourite device of Shakespeare's, to look forward
to the aftermath, **ere the set of Sun . . . upon the Heath**, a meeting
with Macbeth. When the battle becomes a triumph and Macbeth wins
'Golden Opinions', it is in the context of this baleful opening that we
shall hear of his success, and we shall know that a struggle of another
kind is to be fought. To the tumult of the storm are added now the
imperious cries of the familiars summoning the dependent Witches—
the wail of the cat **Gray-Malkin**, the croak of **Paddock** the toad,
and perhaps the shriek of an owl. There is no doubt that the owl plays
an important part in the atmosphere of the play: this bird of ill-omen
shrieks at the moment of Duncan's murder (II.ii.4, 17); indeed, Lenox
hears its clamour all night long (II.iii.65 f.); a 'Mousing Owl' is among
the unnatural portents observed by the Old Man (II.iv.13). In IV.i.3
the third Witch's familiar is called 'Harpier', a name which suggests
a bird of prey. This treatment of the play's opening scene involves a
departure from the Folio lineation. In the Folio, the first Witch calls
to Gray-Malkin, and the line which follows runs thus:

All. Padock calls anon: faire is foule, and foule is faire . . .

Most editors agree that some redistribution of the lines is necessary
and that, while 'Padock calls' is the cry of the second Witch, the third
Witch answers 'anon' (I am coming) to the call of her familiar spirit.

This short scene has a strong rhythmical pulse, a doggerel grotesque
and sinister, never laughable, which is sustained against the violence
of the back-stage noise. The words of the Witches emphasise this
violence and spring from it, and they reach their climax in that utterance of incantatory unison which is the first suggestion given to us
of an upsetting of the moral order:

Fair is foul, and foul is fair.

*   *   *

[I.ii.1-45]   Their voices, and even the thunder, are drowned in the din of battle: there is no pause in the sequence between Scene One and Scene Two. The *Alarum within* (shouts and groans, the clash of weapons, the beating of drums, the discordant blasts of trumpets, the 'double Cracks' with which we are told in metaphor that the cannons are 'over-charg'd') is the playhouse equivalent of the battle itself. Shakespeare is reserving for his last Act the visible representation of combat on the Stage.

King Duncan enters, accompanied by *Malcome, Donalbaine, Lenox, with attendants, meeting a bleeding Captaine*. The entourage emerges from one of the great Doors of the Stage, as from the royal head-quarters: the noise of fighting will accordingly be outside the other Door, and the Captain, who has come straight from the battle, will enter from that side. His appearance is given immediate definition (in the manner of the poetic drama) by the King's opening question: **What bloody man is that?** and his part in the exposition of the play is prescribed for him:

> **he can report,**
> **As seemeth by his plight, of the Revolt**
> **The newest state.**

The 'Hurly-burly' then is a revolt against the King. The sight of the *bleeding Captaine* presents in visible terms the image of blood which pervades the play. The wounded soldier is not yet at pains to show us how faint he is, how his 'Gashes cry for help': his words are energetic and, though critics have attacked the style of his speeches as crude and bombastic, it is likely that Shakespeare used it deliberately as highly effective for its purpose. Coleridge pointed out that these speeches of the Captain may be compared in language and rhythm with the Player's speeches in HAMLET, II.ii; in both cases 'the epic is substituted for the tragic', both passages are rhetorical and highly-coloured battle narratives, and there is some rather close correspondence of detail. There is, therefore, reason to suppose that the style was chosen to fit the purpose of both speeches. In this case, Shakespeare's intention is that the sensational words and elaborately vigorous mime of his actor should represent (take the place of) the battle, in its unfinished state: **Doubtful it stood**. The metaphor of the **two spent Swimmers** clinging together is underlined, as he hangs heavily for a moment round the neck of one of his supporting soldiers. But then he cuts loose, to create for us the formidable danger of **the merciless Macdonwald** with his muster of **Kerns and Gallowglasses** from **the Western Isles**. But while **Fortune** smiles on the rebel, **brave Macbeth** (it is significant that the first of his personal qualities to be stressed in the play is his physical courage) disdains Fortune and conquers as **Valour's Minion**. Again in violent mime the Captain enacts Macbeth's heroism, and shows us how he

> **carv'd out his passage,**
> **Till he fac'd the Slave:**

the moment of suspense, when the two warriors confront each other, is marked in the Folio by the short line. And besides his expository function, the speaker shows a lively individual personality; there is a grim and ironical relish, coming well from the brave Captain, in the very idea of such polite formalities preceding such gruesome slaughter:

> **Which nev'r shook hands, nor bade farewell to him,**
> **Till he unseam'd him from the Nave to th'Chops,**
> **And fix'd his Head upon our Battlements.**

The jubilation which greets the graphic enactment of this frightful blow is quickly quenched by the sombre account of the Norweyan Lord's **fresh assault**. Again the lively personality of the Captain emerges in the dour irony with which he speaks of the **skipping Kerns** and his sardonic humour in rebutting the suggestion that the new danger could dismay Macbeth and Banquo:

> **Yes, as Sparrows, Eagles; or the Hare, the Lion.**

His speech gathers force with the crescendo of the battle, but the

vigour of his rebuttal taxes his strength. After **I cannot tell** there is
a metrical gap, and he seems to fail in mid-sentence:

> **but I am faint,**
> **My Gashes cry for help.**

The last line of his speech is a short one; the onlookers run to support
him and, as he is helped out (leaving the King, and us, in uncertainty
about the issue of the rebellion), Duncan begins a new and regular
line.

[46-69]   While the Captain is led to the King's headquarters, the
Thanes of Rosse and Angus enter from the other Door, beyond which
we have heard the noise of fighting. They make a breathless entry:

> **What a haste looks through his eyes!**

Rosse, as he continues the account of the battle, uses the present tense,
as if the threat of disaster still overhung the King's army:

> **—Whence cam'st thou, worthy Thane?**
> **—From Fife, great King,**
> **Where the Norweyan Banners flout the Sky,**
> **And fan our people cold.**

We are held in suspense, not because the Thane of Rosse is fond of
playing cat-and-mouse with his hearers, but because Shakespeare is
dramatising the battle in all its phases, and quite deliberately and very
skilfully holding up the climax. We hear now how first **Norway**
himself and then **that most disloyal Traitor The Thane of Caw-**
dor revived the battle which had seemed to end with the death of
Macdonwald: once again Macbeth is presented as the Homeric hero
of this hurly-burly:

> **Till that Bellona's Bridegroom, lapp'd in proof,**
> **Confronted him with self-comparisons,**
> **Point against Point, rebellious Arm 'gainst Arm,**
> **Curbing his lavish spirit: and to conclude,**
> **The Victory fell on us.**

And as Rosse brings to a close his account, the trumpets blow for victory, resolving in a triumphant cadence the jarring discords of battle.

From this scene there emerge two significant features of the stagecraft of Shakespeare's poetic drama. Neither time nor place is to be considered literally. The scene begins with the direction *Alarum within*: fifty lines later, after a temporary success and a grave and menacing renewal of the rebel onslaught, the King's army is pronounced victorious, and we hear that the Norweyan King **craves composition**. We are not to think that the battle ceases after the opening alarum: the battle is continuous in the narrative description of both speakers, and the phases of the story are no doubt punctuated by further alarums, until the final trumpet crowns the announcement of victory. By the same token, we are not to think of a realistic setting for the scene: we are not to imagine the Door from which the King emerged as the entrance to his tent. Instead, in our mind's eye, we are on the battlefield. Since the Captain, instead of remaining in character as a wounded soldier, near to fainting, himself enacts the heroism of Macbeth in the heart of the combat, and since Rosse shows us by posture and gesture and the tone-colour of his voice the succession of images which lead up to victory—the Norweyan banners, the Thane of Cawdor, and, as climax, Bellona's bridegroom—the focus of our attention throughout most of the scene is upon the battlefield, and the action of the scene is the battle itself rather than Duncan's reception of the news. We are made vividly aware of the loyal heroism of the protagonist and of his King's gratitude and unfaltering trust: the contrast with rebellious treachery is quite clearly stated:

> **No more that Thane of Cawdor shall deceive**
> **Our Bosom interest: Go pronounce his present death,**
> **And with his former Title greet Macbeth.**

I'll see it done, says Rosse, and the King clinches the matter with his rhyming line:

> **What he hath lost, Noble Macbeth hath won.**

At the end of the scene, Rosse and Angus go back the way they came, to 'see it done'. The King and the rest of his entourage go by the other Door, returning to headquarters. As they depart, *Thunder*, and the opening of the Study-curtains, plant us immediately upon the heath, as the Witches promised us we should be 'ere the set of Sun'.

*   *   *

[I.iii.1-37] A gaunt and stricken bush in the Study, the revival of the storm, and the appearance of the Witches themselves combine to transform the whole Stage into wild open country: Macbeth will reinforce this effect when, later in the scene, he describes the encounter as taking place 'upon this blasted Heath'.

We now see the Witches at close quarters. Whereas before they were remote creatures of the air, they are now in our midst, earthy hags with a petty malignity, spitefully revengeful. It is the appropriate moment to consider what impression these Witches make as they appear on the Stage of the Jacobean playhouse. According to Holinshed, 'the common opinion was, that these women were either the weird sisters, that is (as ye would say) the goddesses of destinie, or else some nymphs or feiries, indued with knowledge of prophesie by their necromanticall science, bicause everie thing came to passe as they had spoken.' Shakespeare adopts Holinshed's epithet 'weird'; this word, when used as a noun, meant 'fate' or 'destiny'; as an adjective, it indicates that the Witches regard themselves as instruments of Fate, or perhaps that they are able to foresee the destinies of men. But, although Shakespeare's Witches are in some sense instruments of Fate, they are not at all like goddesses of destiny or nymphs or fairies. They bear instead some resemblance to Samuel Harsnet's 'true *Idea* of a Witch, an olde weather-beaten Croane'.[2] But Harsnet's witch is a harmless, even absurd old woman, who can inspire fear only in the superstitious. Shakespeare's dramatic purpose led him to present a kind of witch different from Holinshed's stately goddesses, but it is also true that his purpose was different from that of the sceptic Harsnet. While his conception contains elements of both, it is not wholly like either. Shakespeare's Witches present, as Coleridge noted, 'a sufficient resemblance to the creatures of vulgar prejudice to act immediately on the audience'.

He has painted them according to popular belief in that he surrounds them with traditional paraphernalia. They are 'wither'd', and 'wild in their attire', they have 'choppy' fingers and 'skinny Lips', and 'Beards'—it is by this last sign that Parson Hugh (THE MERRY WIVES OF WINDSOR, IV.ii.206 f.) claims to recognise a witch: 'I think the 'oman is a witch indeed: I like not when a 'oman has a great peard.' Among the targets of Harsnet's mockery is the belief that the malice of witches led them to kill or bewitch domestic animals, that **Killing Swine** was among their favoured pastimes: 'Why then ho, beware, looke about you my neighbours; if any of you have a sheepe sicke of the giddies, or an hogge of the mumps, or an horse of the staggers . . . then no doubt but mother *Nobs* is the Witch.' It was held too (the authority is King James I in his *Daemonologie*, which was published in Scotland in 1597, and appeared in England in 1603) that for their revenge they learnt 'to joint dead corpses, & to make powders thereof'—much virtue in 'a Pilot's Thumb'. It is no goddess that assumes the form of 'a Rat without a tail'. However, the traditional witch also possessed less material powers: she could 'rayse stormes and tempestes in the aire, either upon Sea or land', and 'thicken & obscure so the air' as to become invisible in it. Shakespeare's Witches possess these powers too: and certainly in their effect on Macbeth and Banquo there is an element of mystery or fear: they 'look not like th'Inhabitants o'th'Earth'; they have 'more in them, than mortal knowledge' (I.v.3); they provoke 'cursed thoughts' (II.i.8, 20—Banquo who 'dreamt last Night of the three weird Sisters' implores the merciful powers to restrain in him 'the cursed thoughts That Nature gives way to in repose'). They are, to this extent, personifications of the power of evil, as well as (in White's phrase) 'vulgar Scotch witches, smelling of snuff and usquebaugh'.

It is not therefore surprising that their exercise of the powers of evil, to begin with at least, takes the form of petty malice, of personal spite. The short story of the **Sailor's Wife** who is so reckless as to call a witch a witch, and is duly punished through the person of her husband, is told with as much intensity as that of the Ancient Mariner himself. The expert miming of Dick Cowley, or whichever of the company's comedy gang played the part (Baldwin believes that

Cowley played the part of the Old Man), gives life to the munching of chestnuts, the insulting rebuff, the sailing in a sieve, the mariner's insomnia which makes him dwindle, peak and pine. The curse upon the pilot not only shows the malice of the Witches; it is also integral to the structure of the play. Their evocation in words of another storm, a bark **Tempest-tost**, combines with thunder and wind-machine to create the storm in the playhouse; their sentence upon the **man forbid** who will 'sleep no more' begins a series of insomniac images which pervade the play. As her sisters huddle round the first Witch and she raises on high her trophy of a pilot's thumb, the word 'homeward' has a special emphasis of malice:

> **Here I have a Pilot's Thumb,**
> **Wrack'd, as homeward he did come.**

The threat to the mariner's voyage is in deadly earnest. As it reaches its climax, the distant rattle of a side-drum picks up the rhythm of the jingle, and the third Witch answers it:

> **A Drum, a Drum:**
> **Macbeth doth come.**

The sound of the *Drum within* grows in volume, and the irregular doggerel of the scene's opening resolves itself into an incantation in strict rhythm of four beats to a line:

> **The weird Sisters, hand in hand,**
> **Posters of the Sea and Land,**
> **Thus do go, about, about . . .**

Thrice the Witches dance to each of their familiar spirits. Their 'going about' marks a circle in the very middle of the Stage between the Stage-Posts, a magic circle into which their victim is to be lured:

> **Peace, the Charm's wound up.**

The words are spoken in a moment of silence, before the storm breaks again; and they retreat into a remote area of the perimeter outside the Stage-Posts, where they lurk in close proximity to the groundlings, but seemingly at a distance from the victim who is to appear at the farther Door.

[38-88] And from that Doorway come two soldierly figures, still armed for battle, booted and muffled in their great riding-cloaks against the force of the contrary wind.[3] Their miming—a routine part of the accomplishment of the King's Men—and the first words that we hear bring back the full fury of the storm to mark this significant moment. Throwing his cloak off his face, the leader of the two clamours with all his lungs in the teeth of the gale:

So foul and fair a day I have not seen.

There is a conqueror's exultation in Burbage's cry, and bravado too; and we do not miss the echo of the Witches' perverse incantation, 'Fair is foul, and foul is fair'. With this use of clear verbal echoes Shakespeare often points the irony of a situation.

But it is Banquo who now gives added life and atmosphere to the bare scaffold of the Globe. His shout, with cupped hands, from the area of the Doorway, **How far is't call'd to Forres?**, creates the illusion of distance across the front of the Stage (through the filthy air) to where the Witches huddle beyond the far Post. And he describes them to us, as is necessary in the conditions of this theatre:

What are these,
So wither'd, and so wild in their attire . . .

and he prompts our interpretation of them:

That look not like th'Inhabitants o'th'Earth,
And yet are on't?

Banquo's elaborate description of the appearance and behaviour of the Witches is an essential element in Shakespeare's stagecraft. The sense of mystery gathers about them: if they are not creatures of this world, it may not be lawful, or even possible, to **question** them. At any rate, they lay their **choppy** fingers on their lips, as if they may not speak to Banquo. Their mission is first to Macbeth. Macbeth stalks straight into the trap that is set for him, with his bold challenge:

Speak if you can: what are you?

He steps unknowingly into the charmed circle which they have prepared, and he is standing there at the moment when he receives their triple salutation. **Glamis** he accepts with an ironically courteous bow, **Cawdor** surprises and puzzles him; **King hereafter** causes him to start out of his composure. The verbal statement of this triple theme—marking the three stages of Macbeth's rise to power—is repeatedly emphasised in what follows, and it culminates in that moment at the beginning of the second phase of the play when Banquo, surveying Macbeth's royal throne, sums it up, 'Thou hast it now, King, Cawdor, Glamis, all, As the weird Women promis'd' (III.i.1 f.). The first phase of the story—Macbeth struggling to achieve his ambition—is thus verbally presented to us: this is the method of the poetic drama. And it is right that at its first enunciation, it should be presented pictorially as well, with Macbeth in the charmed circle, and the Witches in semi-circle before him, each saluting him by one of the three titles rising in climax from Glamis to Cawdor to King.

Macbeth's reaction to the Witches differs significantly from Banquo's natural and innocent curiosity. Once again it is Banquo who is our interpreter. Macbeth is seen to **start** and seems to **fear** these fair-sounding prophecies; and for the long period of Banquo's questioning and the Witches' answers, he remains in trance-like reverie: **he seems rapt withal**. Macbeth's absorption is worth our attentive notice; it will recur and be marked again by this same word, 'rapt'. While Banquo too questions the Witches, he underlines the dramatic force of the triple salutation: **present Grace** is Glamis, **great prediction Of Noble having** is Cawdor, **Royal hope** is to be King hereafter. His tone is perhaps sceptical:

If you can look into the Seeds of Time,
And say, which Grain will grow, and which will not,
Speak then to me . . .

At least he does not either **beg** their **favours**, or **fear** (Macbeth has seemed to fear) their **hate**. It is not until the Witches have made their riddling answers to Banquo and prepare to depart that Macbeth rouses himself from his trance. As he demands an answer to the question already beating in his mind, we hear again the triple climax:

By Sinel's death, I know I am Thane of Glamis,
But how, of Cawdor? the Thane of Cawdor lives
A prosperous Gentleman: And to be King,
Stands not within the prospect of belief,
No more than to be Cawdor.

In the playhouse we have no leisure to reflect that Macbeth's ignorance of Cawdor's disgrace and defeat is a little surprising.* It is essential to Shakespeare's purpose that Macbeth should be puzzled at the second Witch's greeting; when in a moment he discovers that he is indeed Thane of Cawdor, he will seem to feel that the second Witch has shown supernatural prescience: this will lead him to place his trust in the all-important greeting of the third Witch too. Meanwhile the irony of the situation lies in the fact that we have already heard Duncan's decision to confer Cawdor's former title on Macbeth; while this greeting is incomprehensible to Macbeth, it is perfectly clear to us. Macbeth concludes his questioning in the language of conjuration: **Speak, I charge you**: and *Witches vanish*. Burbage has concentrated first upon one Witch, and then upon another; the illusionist's sleight-of-hand, by which attention is deliberately drawn to one object while another 'vanishes', has made its effect. At the end of his speech they are gone. And the astonishment of the two generals defies us to see through the illusion:

* See *page 22, above.*

—The Earth hath bubbles, as the Water has . . .
—. . . what seem'd corporal,
Melted, as breath into the Wind.[4]

The little dialogue that follows is the first of four such moments when the two speak confidentially to each other. Tantalisingly, the question of Banquo's collusion already begins to arise, although it is no more than a hint. We shall see in the sequel how this question will be resolved:

—Your Children shall be Kings.
—You shall be King.

But Macbeth shies away from the dangerous suggestion:

And Thane of Cawdor too: went it not so?

and in Banquo's crisp answer the momentary tension is dissipated:

To th'self-same tune, and words . . .

[88–156] **Who's here?** Angus and Rosse have been sent by the King to greet Macbeth. The logic of the narrative, therefore, demands that they enter by the Door opposite to that by which Macbeth and Banquo entered on their way from the battle. We know the news they bring, and it has been pertinently brought to mind by the dialogue immediately preceding their entrance: Macbeth is to be given the title of Thane of Cawdor. The moment of this announcement, significant as it is, is deliberately postponed while the messengers recreate in formal verse the valour of Macbeth and the gratitude of the King. And when the moment comes, it comes with the additional force of an incisive irony:

And for an earnest of a greater Honour,
He bade me, from him, call thee Thane of Cawdor . . .

We hear no more of the 'greater Honour' promised by Duncan, but this phrase serves to remind the audience (and Macbeth) that, if the Witches are to be believed, the gift of Cawdor's title is a pledge that Macbeth will soon be King. Expecting the announcement, we are able to focus our attention on Macbeth's reaction to it—and Banquo's:

What, can the Devil speak true?

Banquo is spontaneous and astonished: Macbeth is cautious: his question, **Why do you dress me in borrowed Robes?**, introduces what will prove to be one of the pervasive images of the play—that Macbeth's honours are 'borrowed Robes' which do not fit him.[5] The question seems to expect, and gets, a rational explanation. Angus's answer (implicitly ironical in its recognition of the former Thane of Cawdor's treason) is profound in its effect upon Macbeth, who sees only the fulfilment of the prophecy contained in the Witches' second salutation. To emphasise this moment, Burbage uses the great depth of the Globe Stage. Rosse and Angus remain close to the Tiring-House façade, Banquo momentarily with them; Macbeth moves away from this trio and remembers again the triple theme, given new significance by the **heavy Judgement** on the Thane of Cawdor:

Glamis, and Thane of Cawdor:
The greatest is behind.

As he speaks over his shoulder to Rosse and Angus (**Thanks for your pains**) he beckons Banquo to join him and, confidential in their greater proximity to the audience (in the shelter of a Stage-Post perhaps), they begin the second of their private exchanges. In this dialogue the relationship between them takes a step towards clarification. Macbeth tests Banquo:

Do you not hope your Children shall be Kings . . . ?

Banquo's answer, delivered in Macbeth's ear, is of the profoundest seriousness: he sees at once into Macbeth's concealed thought:

That trusted home,
Might yet enkindle you unto the Crown,
Besides the Thane of Cawdor.

And he warns him solemnly against putting his trust in truth spoken
by the agents of the devil. It is a cardinal theme of the play, and again
and again in the sequel we shall be reminded of Banquo's warning:

. . . oftentimes, to win us to our harm,
The Instruments of Darkness tell us Truths,
Win us with honest Trifles, to betray's
In deepest consequence.

Banquo returns (**Cousins, a word, I pray you**) to Angus and Rosse,
and Macbeth for his all-important self-revelation steps forward to the
perimeter, with the groundlings as his nearest neighbours. **I thank
you Gentlemen** is again thrown over his shoulder to the distant
Thanes.

It is clear that Macbeth has, after all, misunderstood the nature of the
Truths that have been told him. To him they are **happy Prologues
to the swelling Act Of the Imperial Theme**. This is the language
of the playhouse; the metaphor is of the performance of a magnificent
historical play, introduced by a suitable Prologue: in HENRY V just
such a Prologue begs his Muse for 'Monarchs to behold the swelling
Scene'. It seems then that Macbeth is rejecting Banquo's warning; but
in spite of the exaltation with which he at first contemplates 'the
Imperial Theme', his reaction is not the simple one of machiavellian
ambition:

This supernatural soliciting
Cannot be ill; cannot be good.

The short line is slowly spoken, its balanced halves reflecting the conflict of his meditation. As he speaks, we learn the nature of that concealed thought which has been occupying his mind. It is given us
almost in passing:

My Thought, whose Murther yet is but fantastical . . .

and its effect upon him is immense. It is important to realise that in this soliloquy Macbeth is not merely talking about himself, describing (so to speak) his reactions to a sympathetic or curious audience. In the poetic drama the words contain the action. Macbeth at this very moment is convulsed by the **horrible Imaginings** which he speaks of: they are more fearful to him than the palpable dangers (**Present Fears**) of battle. It is true that (as we learn later) he has taken a previous occasion to 'break this enterprise' to his wife. But now at this very moment his hair is standing on end and his heart is knocking at his ribs, and since neither of these phenomena can be shown visually to his audience, the actor conveys the impression by his speech, his posture, his miming: the thought of murder seems to shake his **single state of Man**; the world of the imagination is so strongly absorbing that the world of reality is blotted out of his consciousness: **Function is smother'd in surmise**. Banquo's comment from a distance, **Look how our Partner's rapt** (but a faint echo of the storm that has been raging in Macbeth's bosom among his neighbouring audience), is an indication of how skilfully Shakespeare makes his point clear by verbal (that is, poetical) repetition: he seems rapt withal. . . . Look how our Partner's rapt. And Macbeth himself later writes of this moment to his wife: 'Whiles I stood rapt in the wonder of it. . . .' The verbal link makes it clear to us that this reverie is an extension of that earlier 'start' of fear; the subject of that rapt silence is now developed for us in soliloquy. He has already cherished a dishonourable ambition: the Witches are not so much tempting him, as providing more food for an ambition already nourished by himself.

We recall that Burbage once played the part of Brutus who, like Macbeth, was led by the contemplation of murder into an investigation of his own motives. Macbeth's phrase, 'single state of Man', is a verbal echo of that earlier conflict, and the passage from Julius Caesar (II.i.63 ff.) is so pertinent to the situation of Macbeth that it is worth quoting in full:

Between the acting of a dreadful thing,
And the first motion, all the Interim is
Like a Phantasma, or a hideous Dream:

The Genius, and the mortal Instruments
Are then in council; and the state of man,
Like to a little Kingdom, suffers then
The nature of an Insurrection.

The first movement of MACBETH is devoted to an exposition of this conflict, this 'Insurrection' within the protagonist's 'state of man'.

The soliloquy gives us our first insight into the working of that intense imagination which is one of Macbeth's most remarkable features. As it concludes, we are given another insight. Within Macbeth there is a conflict between ambitious desire and an inertia of purpose. While Banquo from his distance interprets for his companions (in the imagery of **strange Garments**) the struggle in his partner's mind, Macbeth first makes a clear decision against action:

> **If Chance will have me King, why, Chance may Crown me,
> Without my stir.**

Then he postpones all decision:

> **Come what come may,
> Time, and the Hour, runs through the roughest Day.**

The rhyme and the aphorism set a cadence to his reverie, and the scene comes to a swift conclusion. Once again the depth of the Stage makes easy the detachment of Macbeth and Banquo from their fellows. Banquo returns to the centre of the platform:

> **Worthy Macbeth, we stay upon your leisure.**

And Macbeth crosses past him to make his gracious apology to the waiting Thanes. But before they leave, he turns back to Banquo, and we hear the third of their exchanges of confidence:

> **Think upon what hath chanc'd: and at more time,
> The Interim having weigh'd it, let us speak
> Our free Hearts each to other.**

Macbeth asks for open speaking, and Banquo is pleased to agree: **Very gladly**. We are led to anticipate a fourth exchange. The word 'Interim' is a further indication that the passage from JULIUS CAESAR remained in the poet's mind: Macbeth begins now to experience the hideous interim between the acting of a dreadful thing and the first motion. The two generals rejoin Rosse and Angus, and leave by the Door which will take them **toward the King**. The closing of the Study (where that which seemed corporal melted, as breath into the wind) presents us with the bare Stage once again.

*   *   *

[I.iv.1–14] A *Flourish* of trumpets brings Duncan and his train back on to the main Stage by the opposite Door. Where this scene takes place matters not at all. The focus of interest is not geographical but lies in the situation. The continuity of the story is lucid. The end of the previous scene ('Let us toward the King') has prepared us for the coming confrontation. When we last saw the King, he was giving orders for the 'present death' (the immediate death) of Cawdor: now by a natural sequence of events he is inquiring if the sentence has been carried out. Cawdor and his treachery are deliberately recalled to the attention of the audience at this moment, to pave the way for Macbeth's meeting with the King who is to reward him. Malcolm's description of Cawdor's death, reminiscent of the scaffold-scenes which were familiar commonplace to Shakespeare's first audiences,* draws from Duncan an expression of his sense of personal betrayal:

> **There's no Art**
> **To find the Mind's construction in the Face:**
> **He was a Gentleman, on whom I built**
> **An absolute Trust.**

And even as he speaks the words, Macbeth stands in his presence, another such trusted subject:

> **O worthiest Cousin . . .**

* See *page 13, above.*

This hint of a false face which hides the heart is one that we shall hear again.

[15–58] The language of Duncan's speech, and the rhyming couplet which ends it, are formal, as befits a King's greeting to a great subject, but his words are unmistakably heartfelt. In the images of planting and growing, he promises that the honours already bestowed upon Macbeth will increase. In all Duncan's speeches, in his relationship with the other characters, and in all that is said of him by other characters, Shakespeare shows to the audience an unaffected sweetness of nature in the good King, whom Holinshed described as 'a faint-hearted milkesop'. Although the portrait is a small one, it is vivid enough to emphasise the enormity of Macbeth's crime. Macbeth himself is made to seem aware that his treachery is the more frightful in the light of the King's goodness (I.vii.16–25). Baldwin suggests that the part of Duncan was first played by Shakespeare himself. If so, Shakespeare the player will be at pains to give full force to this little episode of the King's emotion. Touchingly overwhelmed with the joy of his victory and the loyal support of his sons, kinsmen and Thanes, he weeps unreservedly:

> **My plenteous Joys,**
> **Wanton in fulness, seek to hide themselves**
> **In drops of sorrow.**

Because he is so much moved, the King is blindly unaware of the danger of his next step, the impulsive appointing of his **eldest, Malcolm** to be his heir (**The Prince of Cumberland** was the title borne by the successor designate of the Scottish throne). Almost in the same breath he invites himself, again by affectionate impulse, to stay at Inverness, in the castle of Macbeth. There is an ironical ambiguity in Macbeth's proposal to **make joyful The hearing of my Wife, with your approach**: a comma after 'my Wife' in the Folio text is a hint of emphasis to the actor: the slightest pause after the words serves to introduce this baleful protagonist to the notice of the audience. Macbeth humbly takes his leave, and while Duncan turns to Banquo, delivers his six lines of menacing soliloquy to his immediate neighbours, the groundlings. Once more the depth of the main Stage makes possible this telling detachment of Macbeth from the other persons of the play. The significance of Duncan's gesture of gratitude at once becomes clear:

> **The Prince of Cumberland: that is a step,**
> **On which I must fall down, or else o'er-leap,**
> **For in my way it lies.**

And as his resolution begins to form, we hear the first of that long series of the images of darkness which will enshroud the afternoon daylight of the Globe in 'thick Night' for so large a part of the play's action:

> **Stars hide your fires,**
> **Let not Light see my black and deep desires . . .**

These images have a powerful cumulative effect of spiritual wickedness, but they also serve the playwright's practical and necessary purpose of bedimming the noontide sun.

After Macbeth's departure the King (with his playful assonance of **Banquo** and **Banquet**) shows us once again his 'absolute Trust'. The cadence is apparently serene, but it is charged with dramatic irony and strikes an important emphasis at this point of the story. As Duncan's initial greeting to Macbeth has told us, King and General are first cousins, and it is this close kinship that has allowed Macbeth to rest in the hope expressed in the previous scene: 'If Chance will have me King, why, Chance may Crown me, Without my stir'—a hope whose fulfilment seemed to be implied in Rosse's suggestion that the gift of Cawdor's title was 'an earnest of a greater Honour'. As Holinshed has it, if Duncan had not declared Malcolm his heir, 'he that was next of bloud unto him should be admitted'. Donalbain later (II.iii.147) sees the danger of this close relationship: 'The near in blood, the nearer bloody.' Shakespeare intends us to shudder, at this last moment of the scene, as the unsuspecting King assures us:

> **It is a peerless Kinsman.**

With a *Flourish* of trumpets the King follows his cousin on the way to Inverness.

*   *   *

[I.v] Slowly the curtains of the Chamber are drawn open, to discover Macbeth's Wife. The upper level of the Tiring-House is the appropriate place for this scene: it is an essentially private scene, an intimate one, the first in the play, in strong contrast to the public nature of all that we have seen hitherto—the re-enactment of the battle, the open country of the 'blasted Heath', the ceremonial welcome of the returning conquerors. The scene involves no more than two players at a time. Moreover the structure of the playhouse reflects the structure of the play: from this beginning in the confinement of her chamber Lady Macbeth embarks upon her long journey to sovereignty, and to it she will return in the aftermath of disillusionment. The suggestion that Lady Macbeth's role begins on the upper level runs counter to the long-established tradition of a star acting part: but when proper deference has been paid to Mrs. Siddons and all her distinguished successors, it should be remembered that the part was written for a boy-player, an apprentice who could be told what the poet wanted him to do, and even chastised—at least with tongue—if he did not do it. The part was well within a boy's compass and needed direct attack rather than subtlety of interpretation. John Edmans, however, was clearly not without skill in subtle characterisation: before his voice was cracked in the ring, Shakespeare was to write for him the part of Cleopatra. As for the complaint that the Chamber was too remote for intense and intimate performance, we should bear in mind constantly the intimate dimensions of the Globe.

[1–31] She stands beside her writing-desk (the 'Closet' of V.i.6?) and reads aloud her husband's letter: from the first words we know that he is describing to her the scene we have already witnessed on the Heath. As we feel the impact of each phase in his story upon her consciousness, so too we hear explicitly stated his reaction to the experience. The inflections of her voice make us sense the urgency of his **I burnt in desire . . .** and the bewilderment of **they made themselves Air.** We remember his strange absorption, **rapt in the wonder of it.**

55

Then comes the cheerful news **Thane of Cawdor**—but more than cheerful, intoxicating, because it was the title by which **these weird Sisters** had already **saluted** him; **and referr'd me to the coming on of time, with 'hail King that shalt be'**. So **Air . . . Cawdor . . . King . . .** are foot-hills rising towards a peak. Macbeth's **my dearest Partner of Greatness** is more than a customary greeting; and it contains both affection and uneasy ambition, carrying 'that suggestion, Whose horrid Image doth unfix my Hair'.

As she lays the letter to her heart, her voice acquires a new range of dynamics. The thoughts of another's mind have come to her simultaneously with (or even later than) utterance of the words: now the words serve, and follow, the thoughts which are her own: we see the difference in her eye, and we hear it in the increased confidence and volume of her voice. The triple theme is once more expressed:

> **Glamis thou art, and Cawdor, and shalt be**
> **What thou art promis'd.**

Her emphatic 'shalt be' gives instant embodiment to her ruthlessness of purpose; and this effect is further strengthened by her contemptuous interpretation of that conflict between ambition and inertia which we have already observed in Macbeth. He is **too full o'th'Milk of human kindness** (he is reluctant to deny his own nature);[6] he would act **holily**. And a new motif is also announced, a verbal chime which will echo through later scenes at moments of dramatic climax: To do or not to do—that is the question. The deed done, then to wish it had not been done. Here are the bare bones of tragedy.

> **Thould'st have, great Glamis, that which cries,**
> **Thus thou must do, if thou have it;**
> **And that which rather thou dost fear to do,**
> **Than wishest should be undone.**

There is emphasis on '*Thus* thou must *do*', but as the verb is repeated, the stress falls on 'fear' and on the negative first syllable '*un*done'. As she imagines herself strengthening his resolution (we shall see how she can **chastise** him **with the valour** of her **Tongue**), the vision of sovereignty, **the Golden Round**, becomes already real to her.

[31-39] She is taken aback by the entry of the servant, and shows involuntary and disproportionate excitement at his news of the King's proposed visit: **Thou'rt mad to say it.** Then she recovers her balance with the practical question **Is not thy Master with him?** The servant is not himself the messenger, but he describes the messenger's breathlessness well enough to give force to Lady Macbeth's metaphorical 'Raven'. Many speeches and phrases in this play are charged with that kind of dramatic irony which the Greek tragedians practised. Now the servant is dismissed with a phrase, innocent to him, but carrying for us a secondary and sinister significance, already anticipated by Macbeth. He was to 'make joyful the hearing' of his Wife with the King's approach; now she expresses that joy: **He brings great news.** John Edmans has been trained so to utter the words that the double meaning is instantly caught by the audience.

[39-55] During her second soliloquy, the structure of the playhouse is again adapted to a dramatic purpose. She points downwards to the main Stage as she interprets in sinister fancy the breathlessness of the messenger:

> **The Raven himself is hoarse,**
> **That croaks the fatal entrance of Duncan**
> **Under my Battlements.**

For in a moment we are to see King Duncan himself, in a mood of serene contentment, walking before his most kind hostess under those very battlements to his doom.

For Lady Macbeth the 'great news' brought by the messenger makes a significant difference. Her dream of sovereignty is now within her grasp: it must not be let slip. There is a metrical pause of powerful effect. 'Between "battlements" and "Come" one syllable is missing. And yet, one of the latest editors of the play . . . holds that "nothing can account for the missing syllable"; to him, the line is "distinctly incomplete". He refers to Steevens's suggestion: "Come, come, you spirits . . ." and to Pope's: "Come, all you spirits". He himself, however, thinks that the reading "ill spirits" ought to be adopted. One wonders whether Shakespeare would be grateful for such collaboration.' (Flatter, *Shakespeare's Producing Hand*, 37 f.) In the hideous invocation which follows her momentary pause, the Lady makes her allegiance clear: she deliberately calls upon the ministers of Hell to strengthen her purpose:

Come you Spirits,
That tend on mortal thoughts, unsex me here . . .

With a favourite touch of bravado, confident in the power of his art, Shakespeare defies his audience to remember that this is a boy-player who is speaking. Instances of a similar assurance are innumerable. The most famous perhaps is Cleopatra's 'I shall see Some squeaking Cleopatra Boy my greatness. . .' There is the same touch of bravado in Portia's promise to 'speak between the change of man and boy, With a reed voice'. Of course the popular device of the girl dressed as a boy depended upon the success of the illusion. Moreover it should be remembered that in an age when the boy-player was the rule rather than the exception, ambivalence of sex, though part of a favourite joke, was a less emphatic feature of this trick of masculine disguise than some modern critics have suggested. When Orsino wonders at the youthfulness of his page Cesario ('they shall yet belie thy happy years, That say thou art a man'), and when Rosalind in her distress caps Oliver's challenge of 'counterfeit to be a man' with 'So I do: but i'faith, I should have been a woman by right', it is essential that we should have no difficulty in accepting that these are women indeed; it is the peculiar pathos of their situations. When they resume their 'woman's weeds', there is no doubt that they are casting off a disguise. In the case of Lady Macbeth, however, Shakespeare's purpose is an unusual one: he makes her renounce her sex: she is to be neither woman nor man, no human being, but the medium of diabolical possession, filled

. . . from the Crown to the Toe, top-full
Of direst Cruelty.

This passage is, in a sense, a continuation of her last soliloquy; she has told us that her husband may prove to be infirm of purpose, and now she seeks diabolical help to prevent her from falling into the same weakness; knowing that Macbeth is 'too full o'th'Milk of human kindness', she begs that her own **Milk** will be transformed to **Gall**. It is no accident that Shakespeare brings Macbeth's hesitancy to our minds by this use of a strong verbal echo. It is clear that Lady Macbeth is to be, at first, more ruthless than Macbeth in the pursuit of ambition; but it is essential to our understanding of her part in the story that we realise the full import of this speech: we are being told that she is deliberately stifling the instincts of **Remorse** and pity, but that does not mean that she is without them. We shall see later how this rejection of her humanity will prove too much for her constancy, and drive her to the brink of madness. Equally it is no accident that Shakespeare makes the Lady deny her nature in the image of the milk of her **Woman's Breasts**. Paradoxically, while she renounces her sex, this image of essential womanhood helps us to accept the illusion of femininity in the boy-player.

With a change in the angle of her head to mark the distinction, she begins another invocation:

Come thick Night,
And pall thee in the dunnest smoke of Hell . . .

Once again a strong reminiscence knits tight the texture of the play. Like her lord (I.iv.50 ff.), Lady Macbeth calls on darkness to hide the deed, but in terms of her own diabolical allegiance; and in her fear lest the **compunctious visitings of Nature** should shake her purpose, she draws **the Blanket of the dark** against the eye of **Heaven** itself. As with the sharp objectivity of his incisive voice (learnt perhaps for Regan last year) he speaks of **my keen Knife**, Edmans leaves us in no doubt that Lady Macbeth at this moment intends to use that instrument herself. In the manner of the poetic drama, the deed is imaginatively presented to us, here and now, and a gesture, the fingers closing on the hilt of an imagined dagger, underlines the force of her words.

[55–74] Her jubilant salutation repeats the familiar triple theme: **Glamis . . . Cawdor . . .** (again the climax is deliberately veiled) **the all-hail hereafter**. But as Macbeth opens his mouth to speak, the troubled rhythm of statement and question halts the music. **My dearest Love** is an affectionate greeting from the husband safe home from the wars. Then the pause is too long for innocence. **Duncan comes here tonight**. Her question comes pat on the cue: **And when goes hence?** and Macbeth's **Tomorrow** is quick too: then again the hesitation that betrays the guilty heart: then **. . . as he purposes**. All this with muted voices; but her savage outburst

> **O never,**
> **Shall Sun that Morrow see . . .**

has full and decisive tone. She stops short, with her line incomplete, as the Folio's lineation makes clear: and in the long silence (nearly half the length of the line) Macbeth from his lofty position on the upper level stares outwards to the audience: when she speaks again, it is in the resumed regularity of smooth pentameters that she interprets for us (as in the subdued light of the daylit theatre is often necessary) the guilt and hesitation expressed on his countenance:

> **Your Face, my Thane, is as a Book, where men**
> **May read strange matters.**

And, the metre still flowing regularly, she calms his nerves, counselling him in the practice of deception:

>   **To beguile the time,**
> **Look like the time.**[7]

The sinister images of **th'innocent flower** and **the Serpent under't** will invest later scenes with more vivid colour in reminiscence.* Another example of Greek irony underlies the phrase **He that's coming, Must be provided for**: it has been anticipated by Duncan, the

---

* See *page 13, above.*

unknowing victim, himself, in his expectation of the 'welcome' await-
ing him (I.iv.56 f.). It is the hostess's duty to provide for her guest, to
administer the **great Business** of a royal visit, but the menace implied
in her words is unmistakably clear, and made the clearer by the
ambiguity of her chosen word **dispatch.**

In her confident certainty she slips into the ringing finality of rhyme:

> **Which shall to all our Nights, and Days to come**
> **Give solely sovereign sway, and Masterdom.**

The assurance is momentarily checked by Macbeth's temporising
evasion:

> **We will speak further.**

But the rhyme is insistent:

> **Only look up clear:**
> **To alter favour, ever is to fear.**

Her cadence (after the couplets a metrical post-script) makes even more
explicit the hints contained in 'my keen Knife' and 'my dispatch':

> **Leave all the rest to me.**

Clearly she means to murder Duncan herself.

*   *   *

[I.vi.1–10] On the closing of the Chamber-curtains, there follows
immediately a brief spell of delight (scarcely a dozen lines)—the only
such in the play. The swift continuity which is native to Shakespeare's
playhouse makes possible this telling juxtaposition of moods. We shall
recall Duncan's pleasure in this scene, when we hear of him at bed-
time being 'shut up in measureless content'. The words rest with
Duncan and Banquo, but all those on the stage contribute to the atmosphere. The Folio specifies *Hoboyes, and Torches.* The tune on the haut-

boys ambles; the torches suggest dusk at the end of a day's hard journey; the cavalcade (who have just dismounted from their horses, and are therefore walking the last stretch in their riding-boots) come in ambling like the music. They are not within sight of Macbeth's house till they reach the nearer Stage-Post: rounding it, they catch their breath in delight at the first view of **this Castle** with its **pleasant seat**. This castle is of course the façade of the Tiring-House, and Shakespeare has felt the need for his ironical purpose to invest the familiar architecture with an atmosphere of charm and homely peace. The effect of contentment is none the less vivid because of the latent irony. Banquo's little excursion into nature-study should not prompt us to read into his character a significant interest in ornithology: Lowin is here not expressing character, but suggesting atmosphere, and for this purpose he bends all his skill of speech to make us sense the imagery of wholesomeness and affection; of hospitable welcome (the **Guest of Summer** feels contentment in **his loved Mansionry**); of the security in which the birds find the fulfilment of their love, make their **pendent Bed** and **procreant Cradle**. And with his skill of mime Lowin makes us see **the Temple-haunting Martlet**, the house-martin, dart with its swooping flight to find its nest amid the projecting stones of the castle-wall. His companions follow the bird's path and see others in flight. The façade of the Tiring-House is transformed by their miming and the poet's words.

[10–31]   We are allowed a mere ten lines of this happy mood: for from the farther Door comes forth **our honour'd Hostess**, looking like the innocent flower. It is significant of the way in which this close-knit drama is built that the words **Hostess** and **Host** and **Guest** are insistently emphasised in this little scene, which began with the 'Guest of Summer'. The motif is continued in the sequel, and at every mention the irony of the King's content is stressed. The substance of the scene, its part in the course of the story, is the reception of the King by his seemingly loyal subjects, the entertainment of a guest by his host and hostess. The double relationship of King–subject, Guest–Host is to be underlined almost immediately by Macbeth himself. When Lady Macbeth speaks of **the late Dignities**, she means the title of Cawdor, and she is making a separate, special acknowledgement of this new honour: so too when Duncan asks **Where's the Thane of Cawdor?**, there is a playful grace about this unfamiliar address. **By your leave Hostess**—the King precedes his subject, the victim his executioner. As Duncan makes his 'fatal entrance' under the battlements of Inverness, so close is the continuity of the play in the conditions of the playhouse that we hear still the echo of Lady Macbeth's sinister jest about the croaking raven, which she made as she stood on the upper level looking down on to the main Stage. It is to be noticed, by the way, that the word **love** is used five times in this short scene, but never by Lady Macbeth.

*   *   *

[I.vii.1–28]   *Ho-boyes.*   *Torches.*
Enter a Sewer, and divers Servants with Dishes and Service over the Stage.
Then enter Macbeth.

Just as the setting of the previous scene was at the Castle-Gates, so now the necessity is that we should be, as it were, 'outside the banquet-hall'. The machinery for this is simple: the Folio has given us explicit instructions. The Hautboys strike up once more, beyond one Door, a brisker tune. From the opposite Door come the torch-bearers, the *Sewer* (that is, a major-domo, a steward), and the servants with their sumptuously laden dishes. Whatever activity—whether comic or business-like—accompanies the appearance of this gang, their dramatic purpose is clear, to establish for us the fact, and the direction, of the banquet with which the King's arrival is being celebrated. (Incidentally we hear later on, from the Porter, that below stairs the celebration was continued until 'the second Cock'.) The little procession makes for the Door opposite to its entrance, for that quarter from which the music and the sounds of revelry, which indicate the royal banquet, are heard. Economically the necessary locality of the scene has been established.[8] The banging of a door off-stage, and the sudden cessation of the sounds, provide an effective spring-board for Macbeth's swift entry: he has left the banquet, to be alone with his disquieting thoughts.

The speed of his entry brings Burbage straight to the front of the Stage, the hub of the Wooden O, and he raps out his opening sentence:

**If it were done, when 'tis done, then 'twere well
It were done quickly.**

Three times in Macbeth's torrential sentence the key-word 'done' is
sounded, but the emphasis falls heavily on the first of the three, and
then with equal weight on the need to act 'quickly'. Lady Macbeth
has already observed her husband's struggle between reluctance and
ambition: she has noted the distinction implied in 'that which rather
thou dost fear to do, Than wishest should be undone'. Once again
the question is presented—to do or not to do. Beginning thus with a
significant verbal echo, the struggle is now intensified. We have no
need to ask what the **it** of the opening line is. The subject-matter of
this whole soliloquy is **the Deed**, and the outrage of it is evoked for
us with as much intensity as if it were already done. The speech is no
noble philosophical speculation, no companion-piece to Hamlet's 'To
be or not to be'. Starting with an impulsive longing to have done with
the deed, Macbeth proceeds to a cynical reckoning of the odds. There
is nothing admirable about his willingness to risk eternal damnation:
his conscious obsession with retribution in this world is expressed in
emphatic iterance of the word 'here': his fear is that the murder will
not be

> **. . . the be-all, and the end-all, here,
> But here . . .**

The Folio prints a full-stop between **end-all** and **here**, not to indicate
the end of a sentence, but to mark this emphasis and a strong pause
before the verse gathers speed. And the iterance continues:

> **We still have judgement here . . .**

But the matter of retribution is not all. With a shift of position, Burbage marks a change of tone: a backward glance at the Door which
leads to the banquet-room brings the picture of the King, content
with his hospitable welcome, before our mind's eye:

> **He's here in double trust . . .**

The motifs of **Subject** and **Host** revive the carefully established ironies of the previous scene. But over and above these considerations of kinship and duty, **strong** as they are **against the Deed**, Duncan's **Virtues** are acknowledged as a further deterrent: it is not Holinshed's 'milkesop' who

> **Hath borne his Faculties so meek; hath been**
> **So clear in his great Office.**

There is no direct suggestion that Macbeth himself is consciously moved by pity for Duncan, but rather that he is afraid of the effect of his **horrid deed** on the rest of the world; a universal outcry against the murderer of Duncan is part of the **Consequence** he fears. But at this point the language of the speech undergoes an astonishing intensification. We are lifted off this earth to the transcendental images of **Pity . . . Striding the blast . . .** and **Heaven's Cherubin, hors'd Upon the sightless Couriers of the Air.** And the heightened imagery is accompanied by a heightening through alliteration of the verbal music (the deliberate use of a familiar device is remarkable: **Trumpet-tongu'd . . . deep damnation . . . naked New-born-Babe . . . the blast . . . Heaven's Cherubin, hors'd . . .**). During these last ten lines he suffers in imagination the world's opinion of the horror of his deed, and this Shakespeare achieves through means possible in no other medium than the poetic drama. Although Macbeth is not, it seems, consciously prepared to accept morality as a guiding principle, we feel in this highly charged poetical climax a deep natural reluctance in him, an imagination intensely stirred, a crisis of compunction unrecognised by himself. The great climax, with its falling cadence of **tears shall drown the wind,** is followed by a reaction of hesitant uncertainty; **I have no Spur** is growled in spiritless anti-climax; and the indeterminate half-line, **And falls on th'other,** suggests that his sentence is interrupted by a renewal of the sounds of revelry and music, as the door of the imagined banquet-room is momentarily open for Lady Macbeth's entry. The unseen door slams, and the banquet is once more inaudible.

[28–82] But her first words to him remind us that the banquet still continues; we are not allowed to forget the near presence of the King in the urgent dialogue which ensues. Lady Macbeth is at first concerned with the suspicious oddity of her husband's behaviour: **Why have you left the chamber?** Macbeth, it seems, has come at last to a firm decision:

We will proceed no further in this Business.

The justification he feels it necessary to give for his retreat is the conclusion of his soliloquy. He once more expresses his deep-seated reluctance, this time in terms of his own reputation. We have seen earlier in the play how he has **bought Golden Opinions**: again his new honours are expressed in the imagery of new garments, and Lady Macbeth sarcastically picks up the metaphor: **Was the hope drunk, Wherein you dress'd your self?** Just as his hesitation is an echo of earlier scenes, so her indignation recalls her decision to stiffen his resolve. She is here, it emerges, to chastise with the valour of her tongue all that impedes her husband from the golden round (I.v.28 ff.): glancing backward and forward, from scene to scene, the poet weaves the texture of his play very close. Her eloquent persuasion is highly evocative: she summons to our mind's eye the scathing picture of the drunkard hope, who wakes the morning after his carousal, to look **green, and pale**. (Her metaphor is the more vivid after the intermittent bursts of revelry we have heard from off-stage.) Macbeth is Valour's minion; his Wife, ridiculing him as **a Coward**, deliberately chooses the most effective form of attack. To him courage is part of his nature as **a man**, and it is his nature as a man that makes him hesitate. In her answer, that he can show his vaunted manliness only by carrying through their agreed plan, she makes us clearly understand that there was an occasion before the action of the play started when her husband broke this enterprise to her. She has renounced her humanity; the milk of human kindness for which she feels such contempt she has exchanged for gall; and now with a bravado of ruthlessness, sharpened by reminiscence, she ratifies that renunciation, miming, with gesture of nursing at her breast, the horrifying act of dashing out the brains of the **Babe that milks** her. The speech is all the more powerful because the image of the 'naked New-born-Babe' as a symbol of pity is fresh in our minds; Lady Macbeth casts from her not only her baby, but Pity itself.

Under her battery his resolution wavers. The rhythm of the poet's words subtly conveys this moment of failing decision. The Folio prints the passage thus:

> **And dasht the Braines out, had I so sworne**
> **As you have done to this.**
> **Macb. If we should faile?**
> **Lady. We faile?**
> **But screw your courage to the sticking place . . .**

It is possible to rearrange these lines so that they become almost regular pentameters, and most editors have done so. But it should be noticed that, when the first line is naturally delivered, although it is not strictly iambic, it has five clear stresses and there is an opportunity for telling emphasis of the important words. Macbeth's question completes his Wife's unfinished pentameter in equal, hesitant monosyllables: function is once more smothered in surmise. And Shakespeare has deliberately placed her answer, 'We fail?', outside the metrical scheme to add to its strength. This powerful extra-metrical stress conveys the scorn with which she treads down his irresolution. And decisively, as she continues,

> **But screw your courage to the sticking place,**
> **And we'll not fail . . .**

she picks up the pace again, and the plan for drugging the chamberlains is a rising climax of speed and intensity, so as to launch Macbeth on his ecstatic **Bring forth Men-Children only**. As she outlines her scheme, and the picture of the bloodied chamberlains takes shape, so the poet is beginning to build up the image of the King's chamber where the murder—the central act of the play's first movement—is to take place. This episode, which began in reminiscence, grows into anticipation. But now, irresolution conquered, Macbeth without conscious irony gives to his Wife the advice she has given to him: he echoes her very words, 'to beguile the time, Look like the time':

Away, and mock the time with fairest show,
False Face must hide what the false Heart doth know.

With the appearance of formal gaiety (serpent beneath the innocent flower), they take hands like partners moving to the dance, and go towards the banquet-hall: at the appropriate moment, the unseen door opens for them, and the sound of revelry briefly breaks out anew.

*   *   *

[II.i.1–30] In the silence which follows upon the fading of the sounds of revelry, the Study-curtains open. *Enter Banquo, and Fleance, with a Torch before him.* We have done with the banquet. We are out-of-doors looking up at the night sky. **The Moon is down**, which means that it is after midnight. Moreover there are no stars visible. All this we are told, by Shakespeare's habitual practice, to set the scene for us: the need as usual breeds the opportunity for poetry: and we have a characteristic touch in the charm of Banquo's comparison (playfully spoken, as from father to young son):

There's Husbandry in Heaven,

(they're economising up there)

Their Candles are all out.

Again the posture, miming and vocal inflections of the two figures who come out of the Tiring-House on to the bare Stage create the illusion which the poet is aiming at. The boy Fleance carries a torch in front of his father: the light makes the Stage seem dark—strange paradox. Although the locality is not specified, the illusion of the starless night has been powerfully and economically created.

Out of this darkness emerges a sense of disquiet, again economically contrived. Banquo is reluctant to obey the **heavy Summons** of sleep, fearing **the cursed thoughts That Nature gives way to in repose**. And when he hears footsteps and sees the light of a second *Torch*, in his uneasiness he asks again for the sword which he has just handed to his boy. He has to be reassured that it is only Macbeth, **a Friend**, who is **not yet at rest**. Banquo has just come from the King's bed-chamber: as he speaks, we become aware of the last treads of a staircase visible at the side of the Study, leading to the chamber where **The King's a-bed**. This staircase is, of course, conjectural, but there is no doubt that Shakespeare intended us in the scenes that follow to be constantly aware of the precise locality of the King's chamber; no doubt too that he intended it to be upstairs, as we shall feel when we hear Macbeth speak of his nerve-racked descent (II.ii.18). It would have been possible by the use of mime and gesture for the players to realise Shakespeare's intentions without the luxury of a staircase. In the drowsy rhythm* of Banquo's speech, we feel the **unusual Pleasure** of the King, the generosity of his **Largess**, visibly expressed in the **Diamond** ring which flashes as it is passed from hand to hand. Once more our ears catch the repeated motif of **most kind Hostess**. It is important to Shakespeare's purpose that we should have at this moment a vivid picture in our minds of the King **shut up in measureless content**, completely enclosed round by contentment, as by the curtains of his bed.

The ensuing exchange between Macbeth and Banquo is not overheard by Fleance or the servant. It is the fourth of those four confidential colloquies which began after the meeting with the Witches, and it marks a significant step in the sequence of their relationship. At that first moment of confidence there was the faintest hint of collusion: in the second, Banquo's growing suspicion of Macbeth's design upon the crown led him to utter an emphatic warning against trafficking with the 'Instruments of Darkness': in the third, Banquo received 'very gladly' Macbeth's proposal for an exchange of open confidence, after an 'Interim' in which they could each weigh the issues. Now the interim is passed; the time for open speaking has come. Banquo is direct:

* See *page 24, above.*

I dreamt last Night of the three weird Sisters . . .

(and his words reveal to us what are 'the cursed thoughts That Nature gives way to in repose'):

To you they have show'd some truth.

He harks back to his warning, 'The Instruments of Darkness tell us Truths'. But Macbeth is evasive:

I think not of them . . .

and he asks for a further postponement of open speaking: he sounds his partner with a carefully equivocal proposal, promising **Honour** for some unspecified support:

If you shall cleave to my consent,
When 'tis . . .

and receives what amounts to an unequivocal rebuff: I will take your advice, provided that I lose no honour in seeking to gain these honours you speak of, but keep my soul free from guilt and my allegiance to the King unsullied. Their parting for the night has undertones of mutual distrust.

[31–64] Macbeth's instructions to his servant are matter-of-fact and precise:

Go bid thy Mistress, when my drink is ready,
She strike upon the Bell.

But under the apparent meaning of the words, we hear the more sinister suggestion of a pre-arranged signal. And so Burbage is left alone on the bare Stage—alone in the company of his audience of two thousand, each individual stretched in concentration to share the private disclosures of Macbeth's heart. In the tension of this silence, almost before we are aware of it, the powerful working of that imaginative 'surmise' which, we have seen, smothers 'Function' in Macbeth's kindled mind rises to a new level of intensity. Now it creates an image with, for him at least, an objective reality. Bradley suggested in a well-known passage (*Shakespearean Tragedy*, 352 ff.) that Macbeth's imagination, as it appears in the play, is some sort of substitute for conscience; while this is true, it is not all: to the audience in the playhouse it appears that Macbeth's imagination expresses whatever he feels most profoundly, his fears or his hopes. Later the illusion of menacing voices will express his remorse (or fear), but here the **Dagger**, so far from representing the distant calling of morality, actually expresses Macbeth's black and deep desire: he observes that the dagger marshals him the way he was going; it does not tempt him away from murder, even by the terror which must attend an apparently supernatural vision. The stages of his hallucination are clearly indicated. The position of the 'Air-drawn-dagger' (which, as Lady Macbeth in a later scene tells us, is leading him to Duncan) is fixed for us by the angle of Burbage's gaze and the action of his hand. At first seeing the dagger, he is excited: his clutching is confident: then next moment he wheels round towards the audience and shows a face of consternation. Twice he looks away, and twice his eyes are drawn hypnotically back to the fatal vision. **I see thee yet . . .**: on the first occasion, the dagger seems to marshal him towards his victim: he moves towards the staircase, following it as it leads. **I see thee still . . .**: on the second occasion, the deed is already in imagination done: there are **Gouts of Blood** on the blade and hilt. **There's no such thing** is a determined, and successful, attempt to dispel the illusion.

What follows is a masterpiece of the poet's evocation. At the same time and by the same means he evokes both palpable darkness in his daylit playhouse and spiritual wickedness in the heart of Macbeth. On the bare and unlocalised Stage of the Globe, unhampered by scenic realism, we have that freedom of the imagination which will follow the poet's mind in all its rapidly shifting images:

> **Now o'er the one half World**
> **Nature seems dead.**

The very opening phrase lifts us away from precise locality, and our range of vision is enlarged to the sleeping hemisphere. The **wicked Dreams** suggest Banquo's 'cursed thoughts', the **Curtain'd sleep** recalls Duncan 'shut up in measureless content'. **Pale Hecate's Offerings** bring back to mind the incantation of the Weird Sisters who only just now were winding up their charm on this very Stage. Then Burbage impersonates **wither'd Murther**, hears the wolf-sentinel howl, creeps **towards his design** with **stealthy pace**, then, terrifyingly reminding us of that other night-prowler on his way to the chamber of Lucrece, steps swiftly—**With Tarquin's ravishing strides**—to the foot of the staircase. The silence which has fallen over the one half world adds to the **present horror**: it suits well with Macbeth's bloody purpose. With what seems to be the full close of a rhyming couplet, Macbeth resolves his conflict between hesitant desire and achievement:

> **Whiles I threat, he lives:**
> **Words to the heat of deeds too cold breath gives.**

As if to confirm his resolution, pat on the cue, he hears his Wife strike on the *Bell*, two clinking strokes, which Lady Macbeth remembers afterwards in her nightmare ('One: Two: Why then 'tis time to do't'). At this telling moment, we hear again the chiming of that word which has acquired so special and menacing a significance for us:

> **I go, and it is done.**

And in the lines that follow there is another chime (of **Bell . . . Knell . . .** and **Hell**). The capital letters of the Folio and a comma judiciously placed before the last three words of the cadence throw the rhyme into sharp relief:

> **I go, and it is done: the Bell invites me.**
> **Hear it not, Duncan, for it is a Knell,**
> **That summons thee to Heaven, or to Hell.**

This time the couplet, invoking as it does the powers of Heaven and Hell, is conclusive indeed.

*   *   *

[II.ii] It is to be noticed that in Shakespeare's playhouse a sense of locality is easily set up just when it is needed and relevant, and as easily ceases to have such definition when the need is past. At the beginning of the scene we have just witnessed, the focus was upon midnight under a starless sky, and upon a restless man, reluctant to sleep for fear of 'cursed thoughts'. That particular dramatic need once supplied, we became aware, while Banquo spoke to Macbeth about the sleeping King, of a more precise locality—the bed-chamber on the floor above. As the dagger marshalled Macbeth towards his victim, the locality again acquired definition for us, but during the central passage of the soliloquy we ranged free of time and place in the world of Macbeth's imagination. Gradually 'Tarquin's ravishing strides' and Macbeth's 'steps' upon the 'sure and firm-set Earth' led us back to 'the present horror'; and the sounding of the bell confronted us unmistakably with the time and place of the deed to be done. Now, with the Stage for a moment empty, we are acutely aware of being at the foot of the stairs which lead up to Duncan's chamber; the old King lies there asleep, and we have seen Macbeth go up the stairs, dagger in hand.

[1–15] Then Lady Macbeth slips in from the other side of the Study, a direction which becomes for the time being associated with the private apartments of the host and hostess. Our interest has a dual focus, the duality corresponding indeed to the two levels of the Tiring-House. At one and the same time, we are on the Stage with Lady Macbeth in the tense concentration of her waiting, and picturing with her the scene which is being played out upstairs. Her opening lines, with their balanced antitheses, project both her own fortified confidence and the 'Swinish sleep' of the 'unguarded' Duncan's grooms:

> **That which hath made them drunk, hath made me bold:**
> **What hath quench'd them, hath given me fire.**

No sooner has she voiced her confidence than the screech-owl sets her nerves on edge. The King's Men are adept at mimicry and other sound-effects; at this point the shriek of the owl is as clearly and positively heard from the Huts of the Tiring-House as was the little bell a moment ago. The sound-track of the performance is habitually continuous, dialogue and silence and sound-effects interlocked in deliberately controlled rhythm. This episode of Duncan's murder demonstrates with particular clarity the keenness of Shakespeare's ear. To the hushed and uneasy dialogue on the Stage is added a variety of effects: the clinking of the bell and the silence which follows Macbeth's departure, the shriek of the owl, perhaps the crying of crickets, Macbeth's muffled call and, after a long period of concentration on the words of the actors, the sudden knocking on the door. Moreover again and again the persons on the Stage are made to react in their nervousness to sounds heard or unheard by the audience. This insistence upon the act of listening is part of Shakespeare's deliberate strategy in the creating of tension. Our ears are made sharply aware of the sounds which are significant in the silence of the sleeping house. The strategy begins as early as Macbeth's invocation to the Earth ('Hear not my steps') and his anguished plea that Duncan should not hear the bell. We shall notice with what skill and to what purpose it is developed in the sequel.

Perhaps a clue to Shakespeare's intended rhythm in this passage, not only in words but in the expressive use of silence, underlies the unusual irregularities of the Folio's lineation:

> **That which hath made them drunk, hath made me bold:**
> **What hath quench'd them, hath given me fire.**
> **Hark, peace: it was the Owl that shriek'd,**
> **The fatal Bell-man, which gives the stern'st good-night.**
> **He is about it, the Doors are open:**
> **And the surfeited Grooms do mock their charge**
> **With Snores. I have drugg'd their Possets,**
> **That Death and Nature do contend about them,**
> **Whether they live, or die.**

Modern editors are at pains, by a rearrangement of the lines, to impose a conventional regularity on the metre.

Lady Macbeth is startled (**Hark**) by Harpier's strident cry. Recovering, with a sigh of relief (**peace**), she exultantly greets the omen in a reminiscence of her own signal to Macbeth: the owl is **the fatal Bell-man**, sent (by a custom established in the year the play was first performed) to Newgate Prison to admonish on the eve of their execution persons condemned to die. And we are brought back to the condemned Duncan: she paints more precisely for us the scene in the bed-chamber where Macbeth **is about it**, where **the Doors are open**, where our straining ears do not quite catch the **Snores of the surfeited Grooms**. From up aloft, from the unseen area which has become the magnet of our attention (and hers), comes another sound to set the nerves on edge, a muffled outcry from Macbeth:

Who's there? what ho?

The Folio prints *Enter Macbeth* before this outcry. This may be no more than an indication that he is to speak; but it is conceivable that he appeared for a moment on the upper level (unseen by Lady Macbeth); it is even possible that Burbage's mime, though necessarily brief, gave substance to those lines later in the scene (24 ff.) which describe Macbeth's listening at the door of the 'second Chamber'. Whether or not he appears on the upper level, Lady Macbeth, alone on the Stage, hears him call out and jumps to the conclusion that he has failed, that **'tis not done**; but we shall learn in a moment that his cry followed upon the accomplishment of **the deed** and was provoked by a posthumous alarm. As she again strains to listen for an unidentified sound (**hark**), the mind's ear of the audience is again sharpened, and we are drawn in imagination back to the King's bed-chamber where she has **laid** the **Daggers** of the grooms **ready**. There is a note almost of regret in her impatience (**He could not miss 'em**) and we are reminded that she had intended to kill the King herself: her reason for not doing so is significant, and anticipates her subsequent weakness:

Had he not resembled
My Father as he slept, I had done't.

75

Clearly Macbeth rejoins his Wife on the main Stage at the moment of **My Husband?** It is interesting that, although the Folio has no stage-direction to this effect, it prints these two words as a separate line, in spite of the fact that they make a pentameter with the words that precede them.

[16–58] It is an inevitable feature of the technique of Shakespeare's poetic drama that the execution of the murder should be projected verbally: the motif of the *deed* to be *done* is here at its most intense. There has been a deliberate and rapid accumulation of the echoed words. Lady Macbeth has expressed her fear that ' 'tis not done: th'attempt, and not the deed, Confounds us'; she has told us that, but for an unforeseen access of compunction, she would have 'done't' herself. Now, as her husband returns down the staircase, his hands behind his back, it is with the special force gathered by the iteration of these words that he clinches, in irrevocable finality, the central act of the play's first movement:

I have done the deed.

It is a moment of horror, timeless and isolated. The duet which follows is sustained by a taut musical structure—variations of tempo, alternation of movement and pause, contrast of impatiently prosaic interjections from the Lady with urgent iambic rhythm from Macbeth. The quickfire question-and-answer stresses once again the act of listening in the sleeping house: **Didst thou not hear a noise? ... Did not you speak? ... Hark**. They listen intently, and the focus of interest is shifting to the **second Chamber**, which is aloft, on the opposite side to the King's room; but before Macbeth launches into his distraught account, we are presented with a powerful visible and objective symbol of the irrevocability of the deed: Burbage shows us one of his hands stained with the King's blood—**a sorry sight**. The bloody hand has always been a favourite symbol of murder (as in KING LEAR, III.ii.53); but it is Shakespeare's way, upon occasion, to take such a visible token, invest it with special significance in the dialogue and action of his play, and make it for a time the centre of dramatic interest. Parallel instances are the stocks which embody

Regan's insult to her father's majesty (KING LEAR, II.ii and iv), and the handkerchief which, as Othello thinks, gives visible substance to Desdemona's infidelity (OTHELLO, III.iii and iv, and IV.i). At this point in Shakespeare's story of Macbeth, Burbage's hand provides a visible token of murder which will be verbally intensified in the immediate sequel.

Macbeth scarcely hears his Wife's trenchant rebuke: **A foolish thought, to say a sorry sight.** In this mockery of precise imitative balance she expresses her determination to remain with the urgency of the moment. But he is lost in memory as he relives the minutes after the murder, more real to him than the present danger of his predicament. His fantasy is a reflection of that earlier moment when 'Present Fears' were to him 'less than horrible Imaginings'. Then the murder was 'yet . . . but fantastical'. It is fantastical still, but now in retrospect, and the fantasy is still powerful enough to shake his 'single state of Man', so that 'Function is smother'd in surmise'. Again the imaginative concentration of the audience is at once upon the main Stage and in the unseen area aloft. We are made to share the tension as we hear Macbeth remember how the two sleepers (**Donalbain** and, we presume, since **there are two lodg'd together,** Malcolm) **did wake each other**; the silence of held breath as he **stood, and heard them**; relief as they **address'd them again to sleep.** At the moment of this relief comes a horror greater than the danger of discovery, his realisation that he has alienated himself from God; his **Hangman's hands** are the visible token of the murderer's moral isolation:

> **I could not say Amen,**
> **When they did say God bless us.**

And he passes from reality to fantasy:

> **Methought I heard a voice cry, Sleep no more:**
> **Macbeth does murther Sleep . . .**

His longing for **the innocent Sleep** which he has lost forever floats image by image into his mind. Like the man forbid, the Master o'th'Tiger, unlike the King, shut up in measureless content, who 'sleeps well' for ever (III.ii.23), Macbeth will sleep no more. To his ears, sharpened as they are to an awareness of the smallest sounds, the imaginary voice with its battering iteration seems to cry **to all the House**; and its cry (Burbage recreates it with the full force of his voice) remembers the triple salutation of the Witches, except that the third greeting, of 'Royal hope', is significantly absent:

> **Glamis hath murther'd Sleep, and therefore Cawdor**
> **Shall sleep no more: Macbeth shall sleep no more.**

This passage, with its haunting imagery, is no mere decorative cadenza: it projects for us, more strongly than ever in its contrast with the hushed urgency of what precedes and follows it, the strangely obsessive force of Macbeth's imagination. And, above all, it makes an unforgettable evocation of Sleep itself, **Balm of hurt Minds**, season of all natures. It is an important strand in the texture of the play: at this moment of the murder we begin to feel already the agony of minds that will never again be at peace.

His Wife cannot follow him: her questionings are uncomprehending, earthy, practical, impatient: **What do you mean? . . . Who was it, that thus cri'd?** She interprets the fantasy of his guilt as no more than thinking **brain-sickly**. Her reaction to her husband's bloody hand is also essentially practical:

> **Go get some Water,**
> **And wash this filthy Witness from your Hand.**

As she speaks, he draws his other hand out from behind his back, and she sees with horror that he has brought the grooms' daggers with him. His nerve has gone: once again he is as she painted him in her first soliloquy, **infirm of purpose**, and the business must be put into her dispatch:

> **Give me the Daggers: the sleeping, and the dead,**
> **Are but as Pictures . . .**

There is heroism in her scorn of **the Eye of Childhood** that is terrified of a mere picture; and there is ghoulish bravado in her grim word-play:

I'll gild the Faces of the Grooms withal,
For it must seem their Guilt.

Critics have found a play on words at such a moment distasteful; Coleridge even shuts his ears to it: 'with the exception of the disgusting passage of the Porter . . . there is not, to the best of my remembrance, a single pun or play on words in the whole drama.' Muir rightly observes: 'Those who find it distasteful should read more genteel authors.' While actresses may hesitate to give full force to this word-play, it must be remembered that Shakespeare was working through the broader medium of the boy-players; it was part of their graduation, and his, to develop the use of such quibbling, sometimes as an expression of tense emotion. An elaborate and early example may be found in RICHARD III (IV.iv.362 ff.): Richard is talking to Queen Elizabeth, whose children were the little princes murdered in the Tower by his command:

—Your Reasons are too shallow, and too quick.
—O no, my Reasons are too deep and dead,
    Too deep and dead (poor Infants) in their graves . . .

[58–75] The succession of external sound-effects which was part of Shakespeare's strategy in the earlier part of the scene has for some time been in abeyance, and our attention has been concentrated upon Macbeth's horrified imaginings, upon the Lady's impatience, upon the visible token of the hangman's hands. But now, when Lady Macbeth has moved swiftly up the stairs and Macbeth has been left on the main Stage, the more vulnerable for being alone, the temporarily relaxed alertness of our hearing is again, suddenly, startled into awareness: *Knocke within.* The sound is more purposeful, less incidental, and therefore, it seems, more threatening, than the others we have heard. At first, the knocking is neither unusually loud nor unusually urgent;

why should it be? Those who are knocking, we shall soon discover, are on a mission of no more than everyday importance. But the knocking will grow louder and more insistent as it meets with no response, and the tension generated by it will, therefore, grow, rather than be dissipated by a mere repetition of the same effect. However, though the noise is at first neither loud nor urgent, yet being calculatedly placed thus in the framework of the scene, it comes with a shocking suddenness. The direction of the sound is clearly discernible —beyond the Stage Door opposite that side of the Study where Lady Macbeth entered (from the apartments of the host and hostess) at the beginning of the scene. With the direction of the knocking we will come to associate the world outside the castle.

The sudden sound **appals** Macbeth, and he is appalled, indeed, that so ordinary a sound can appal him. But the spectacle of the bloody hands that seem to **pluck out** his **Eyes** withdraws him again, even at this moment of urgency, from the real world. In the massive imagery of **great Neptune's Ocean** he expresses the hugeness of his guilt: rhythm makes exact reflection of sense, as polysyllabic immensity merges into uniform monosyllables:

> **this my Hand will rather**
> **The multitudinous Seas incarnadine,**
> **Making the Green one Red.**[9]

The significant word that echoes through the ponderous lines (**Hands . . . Hand . . . Hand**) sounds again as Lady Macbeth reappears, and it emphasises the badge of guilt that she too is wearing:

> **My Hands are of your colour . . .**

Her reaction to both the knocking and the blood on their hands is notably different from Macbeth's. To her, the knocking is a reminder only of the need for swift and decisive action. She identifies the direction of the sound: beyond the Stage Door is **the South entry** of the castle. This precise detail is part of the process which brings us back to the real world. And while Macbeth stands tranced in his vision of the incarnadined seas, her sense of urgency finds words in her brief dismissal of the blood on their hands and all its implications:

A little Water clears us of this deed.
How easy is it then!

Her insistence that Macbeth should rouse himself is reinforced by the growing insistence of the knocking; like the visible token of the bloody hands, the knocking has become a focus of dramatic interest, intensified by repetition of the sound (each instance louder than its predecessor) and by iterance in the dialogue (**Whence is that knocking?...** **I hear a knocking ... Hark, more knocking**). As she succeeds at last in drawing him towards that side of the Study which leads to their apartments, **our Chamber,** he turns for a moment at yet another outburst of knocking (the fourth); the importunate sound has marked the return of waking life to the castle, and it wrings from him a cry of despair at the finality of his deed:

Wake Duncan with thy knocking:
I would thou could'st.

And they hurry away. Already we have almost forgotten the victim in our pity for the murderer. The deed cannot be undone: the knocking cannot wake Duncan. This long episode of the murder began with the sound of the little bell, and Macbeth's savagely expressed hope that Duncan should not hear it. It ends with the sound of knocking, and Macbeth's desperate regret that Duncan *cannot* hear it. The sound-effects, with all that they imply in Macbeth's fantastic interpretation of them, are themselves instruments of Shakespeare's dramatic purpose.

*   *   *

[II.iii]   Although the Folio at this point indicates the beginning of a new scene, in practice that continuity which is the particular mark of Shakespeare's playhouse remains uninterrupted. For a moment the Stage is empty, and our attention is solely concentrated on the *Knock-*

ing within beyond the Door; the sound, growing still in volume and urgency, is a bridge, deliberately placed, between the two episodes. What follows is a master-stroke of stagecraft: from the opposite Door (we associate it with the interior of the castle) comes the company's most celebrated comedian, Robert Armin; his first words obliquely— and the keys he carries, directly—establish his role: he is the Porter, the door-keeper, of the castle. This episode of the Porter supplies a need which is partly practical: Macbeth and his Lady must put on their night-gowns and wash the blood from their hands. But this is not just a comic stop-gap. De Quincey, in his famous essay *On the Knocking at the Gate in Macbeth*, observed that this episode increases retrospectively the power of the preceding scene: 'the pulses of life are beginning to beat again; and the re-establishment of the goings-on of the world . . . makes us profoundly sensible of the awful parenthesis that had suspended them.' We realise, with a shock, that while Macbeth was stealing into Duncan's chamber there was carousing below stairs till the second cock. But in the unnatural world of the play it is this everyday episode that is the parenthesis. We have lived through a scene of appalling tension and know that we must experience another equally powerful, though in a different way: the murder has yet to be discovered. Between the two scenes of nightmare, the life of everyday is clearly and economically established for us.

[1–24] Nevertheless, different in tone as the passage is from the context in which it is placed, Armin's Porter is not altogether everyday: like Macbeth, he has a vein of fantasy which absorbs him, and perhaps the vein is as much Armin's as Shakespeare's. It is charged with the grimmest dramatic irony. He drunkenly assumes the role of keeper of **Hell Gate**: the 'joke' is horribly apt, since Macbeth and his Wife have indeed created a kingdom of darkness within the castle. While the knocking continues, Armin in mime creates his caricature of Hell for us, opening his imaginary gate for the grasping **Farmer** whom **th'expectation of Plenty** drove to suicide, the treacherous **Equivocator**, the **Tailor** who turned petty thief: all these creatures of his fancy now join the regicides who already inhabit this Hell; and he lingers with comic relish on his threats of torment: **here you'll sweat for't . . . here you may roast your Goose.** But as he is on the point of admitting a fourth sinner (what will he be?), his fantasy comes to an abrupt end, and we are brought suddenly back to the chilly dawn in the castle (the air that delicately wooed Duncan's gentle senses quite forgotten):

. . . this place is too cold for Hell.

Then Armin shrugs off the role of devil-porter and speaks in his own person directly to the audience. With a shrewd thrust at the whole company, neighbour groundlings, Galleries and all alike—**I had thought to have let in some of all Professions, that go the Primrose way to th'everlasting Bonfire**—he shuffles off in the direction of the knocking: beyond the Stage Door we hear the lifting of chains and drawing of bolts, and for the brief space of time while the gate may be presumed to stand open we catch the sound of a blustering wind outside the castle, which prepares us for Lenox's coming description of the stormy night.

[25–69] The knocking which has come to seem so momentous heralds after all only two Thanes, Macduff and Lenox: the fact that neither is identified by name is unimportant:* to us in the playhouse audience they are early visitors, come to fulfil the King's command to call timely on him. As Macduff light-heartedly indulges the Porter's chatter, the tension of expectancy is stretched near breaking-point. The grim ironies continue: in his dissertation on drunkenness, the Porter unconsciously provides an ironical commentary on that conflict between **desire** and **performance** which has become one of the themes of the play: his observation that **Drink** provokes **Sleep** reminds us that upstairs Duncan's chamberlains, drunk with wine and wassail, still lie in swinish sleep. Above all, his play with the idea of equivocation (as if, ever since he admitted the Equivocator into his hell, the word had been fermenting in his slow fancy) keeps us by iteration verbally in touch with a theme which has its climax only in the last moments of the play.†

When Macbeth reappears (from the Study where he last went), he

---

* See *page 21, above.*
† See *page 13, above.*

seems to have sprung straight from his naked bed: the 'Night-Gown is a house-coat or dressing-gown which he has flung on in a hurry to investigate this knocking in the small hours of the morning: bare feet, bare chest reinforce this effect of emergency. As Macduff makes his unruffled and urbane inquiry, our attention is focused on the floor above. Macbeth's laconic answer is charged with dramatic irony from the knowledge which we share with him alone:

> —Is the King stirring, worthy Thane?
> —Not yet.

Standing at the foot of the stairs, and pointing upwards, the murderer makes imminent the discovery of the murder:

This is the Door.

And Macduff goes alone towards the King's bed-chamber. While Macbeth waits for the inevitable outcry, Lenox's innocent question takes him unawares, and receives yet another ironically brusque answer:

> —Goes the King hence today?
> —He does: he did appoint so.

In contrast with this unforthcoming response, Lenox, a little excitable, feels the need to make conversation with his graphic tale of the **unruly** night. It is the first we hear of the portents that accompanied the unnatural murder of the King. His tale of the dreadful storm, the **Screams of Death**, the dire prophecies, the clamorous owl, again receives but a curt response from Macbeth, whose ears are stretched to catch the first reaction of discovery: yet there is something like relish in the irony of his bald assent to the young man's recital:

'Twas a rough Night.

[**70–153**] The discovery—for all that we have been expecting it—

comes with startling force. Macduff's clamour has a volume of sound we have not heard for many pages of the prompt-book. Lenox runs first up the stairs, Macbeth following with an unnatural hesitation which Macduff has scarcely time to notice, as he shouts for the **Alarum Bell**. The sense of emergency is communicated through his disjointed shouts to the sleeping noblemen, his cries of **awake, awake . . . Murther, and Treason . . . up, up**. But that is not all: his words evoke too the magnitude of that **horror** which **Tongue nor Heart cannot conceive, nor name**; for Shakespeare matches it with the images of sacrilegious violation and the day of judgement itself; the sleepers are to rise up as from their graves; the murder of the King is **the great Doom's Image**. The clamour and the tolling of the great alarum bell (no doubt we see the Porter in the Doorway, pulling at the bell-rope) rouse the household. Lady Macbeth, in her 'Night-Gown' (coming like her husband from their private apartments), is first to answer the summons of the **hideous Trumpet**: but Macduff will not offend the ears of that **gentle Lady**. Banquo is next, almost naked. To him at least Macduff's announcement is blunt:

Our Royal Master's murther'd.

Lady Macbeth's reaction is so prompt as to seem careless:

What, in our House?

And it is tactless enough to be thought callous; this at any rate is implied in Banquo's quick response:

Too cruel, any where.

At intervals the other **sleepers of the House** have come on to the Stage, thronging from that Door which leads from the interior of the castle: the opposite Door, from which we heard the knocking, we associate, in the precise geography of this scene, with the outside world: this association will have an important effect upon the end of the scene. All are in disarray, hair tousled, eyes blinking as if straight from sleep, bare-foot, half-naked. Macbeth comes clattering down the stairs, with Lenox at his heels, and is now in ranting vein, overdoing (so it seems to us who know his secret) the part of the distracted host:

> **Had I but di'd an hour before this chance,**
> **I had liv'd a blessed time: for from this instant,**
> **There's nothing serious in Mortality.**

Macbeth is not consciously speaking the truth; he is trying to deceive his listeners into believing that he is grief-stricken. But at the end of the play we will understand the dramatic irony underlying these extravagant words, when he utters (V.iii.22 ff., V.v.19 ff.) the same sentiments again, and we realise that he was speaking the truth after all; from the moment of Duncan's death his life is empty.

Last of all the sleepers come the King's young sons, bursting out on the upper level of the Tiring-House: again the geography is precise: they are in close proximity to their father's chamber, from which Macbeth 'descended'; in the second chamber, we remember, there were two lodged together. The answers to their terrified questions differ significantly. Macbeth is histrionic, Macduff almost brutally factual, Lenox cautiously sceptical: **Those of his Chamber, as it seem'd, had done't.** Macbeth startles us with the news that he has killed the grooms: and our astonishment is voiced in Macduff's indignant question,

> **Wherefore did you so?**

So we have yet another word-picture of that chamber of death which we never actually see but which is vividly clear to the mind's eye of the audience. But this description is in Macbeth's extravagantly histrionic vein, with its unnatural images: Duncan's bloody skin is cloth of silver interlaced with gold, his wounds are breaches in the wall of a beleaguered city, the naked daggers of the grooms are covered (as if clad in breeches) with blood. It is Macbeth's lurid account of the scene upstairs which causes his Wife to faint: she has after all just seen for herself **His Silver skin, lac'd with his Golden Blood**; and who would have thought the old man to have had so much blood in him?[10] Moreover the killing of the grooms was not part of the plan, a blunder of her husband's for which even her iron constancy is unprepared.

During the commotion of giving first-aid treatment to the Lady, Malcolm and Donalbain hold their brief debate on the upper level. Macbeth's eye is upon them, calculating how they may be brought to serve his purpose; and Banquo's eye is upon Macbeth. On the broad and deep Stage of the Globe the cross-currents of motive and interest are easily emphasised. It is clear that the Princes do not accept Macbeth's convenient identification of the murderers. Malcolm is at first for blurting out their suspicions, but Donalbain, sensing that the murder is the first step in a design upon the throne, feels more acutely the danger to themselves: **Let's away**. After the Lady is carried out, Banquo, determined to **question this most bloody piece of work**, speaks the mind of every honest man:

> **In the great Hand of God I stand, and thence,**
> **Against the undivulg'd pretence I fight**
> **Of Treasonous Malice.**

This uncompromising declaration is the resolution for the time being of that developing relationship between Banquo and Macbeth which we have observed in their four brief and confidential colloquies. Macduff supports Banquo; so do they all. Roused from his rapt thoughts, Macbeth is a moment late in his proposal to **meet i'th'Hall together**. 'This place' which 'is too cold for Hell', and the untimeliness of the alarm which has brought them from their beds, are continually projected for us in the words of Shakespeare's poetical score: the **naked Frailties** of the roused sleepers **suffer in exposure**; they are bidden by their treacherous host to **put on manly readiness**. As they all depart towards the interior of the castle, Malcolm and Donalbain (who have stealthily left the upper level) reappear at the foot of the stairs. Their hurried words of panic are spoken close to the audience, on the perimeter of the Stage. Observing the **unfelt Sorrow**, the **Daggers in men's Smiles**, they have become more certain in their suspicions. It is a kinsman close to the throne who has murdered their father: **the near in blood, the nearer bloody**: and they themselves are in danger. They steal out by the Door through which not long ago Macduff and Lenox entered the Porter's Hell, and which we still associate with the outside world: beyond, we know that the open country (their freedom and safety) lies.

*   *   *

[II.iv.1–41] Since the opening of the play there has been a long, steady gathering of the dramatic intensity. Now we have a brief interlude in which the tension is relaxed, a kind of coda to the play's first movement. The transition of mood is simply made on the Globe Stage. The Study-curtains are shut for the first time since we saw Fleance lighting his father to bed. And now the bare Stage must be invested with a new atmosphere. Gone is the precise locality of the previous scene: no indication is given of our whereabouts, but the emphasis is all upon the morning hour—**by th'Clock 'tis Day**—and the unnatural phenomenon of inexplicable darkness: for there is no daylight—**dark Night strangles the travailing Lamp** of the sun. It may be that the King's Men opened this scene with the sound of a striking clock—perhaps the four quarters and then the brisk and matter-of-fact strokes of eight o'clock. Not only would this mark the passage of time, but also it would give significant emphasis to the portent of unnatural darkness evoked in the dialogue. One of the speakers is, we know, the Thane of Rosse; the other is an Old Man. Just as the locality of the scene remains indeterminate, so too does his identity. Episodes of choric comment are not uncommon in Shakespeare (for instance, in RICHARD III, II.iii; RICHARD II, III.iv; ANTONY AND CLEOPATRA, IV.iii; CORIOLANUS, IV.v.), but the Old Man of MAC-BETH is unusual in that, unlike these citizens, gardeners, sentinels and servants, who are, even in a small way, circumstantially involved in the narrative, he has no part of any kind in the action of the play. His choric function exists in detachment.

His memory stretches back **Threescore and ten** years (a lifetime), but he has never experienced any **dreadful** hour to equal **this sore Night**. He and Rosse peer through the unnatural darkness, and Rosse sums up its portentous implications in the metaphor of the playhouse which is Shakespeare's world, embracing in an upward gesture the familiar canopy that hangs over their heads:

Ah, good Father,
Thou seest the Heavens, as troubled with man's Act,
Threatens his bloody Stage.

The Old Man places **the deed that's done** (the verbal echo ringing unmistakably in our memory) into its proper context of monstrous portents, each reflecting in its own way the horror of the crime—the **Falcon** killed by the **Mousing Owl**, the frenzy of the dead King's horses, **contending 'gainst Obedience**. Unnaturalness, the murderous destruction of dignity, violent rebellion, are all evoked by poetical means.

At the entry of **the good Macduff**, the Old Man withdraws from the conversation of his betters, which is conducted at close range of privacy, and in the veiled language which good men must use in bad times. Macduff's dry factual account of the popular view of what has happened deceives nobody in the audience. His irony is transparent in the bitter tone of his voice: **Those that Macbeth hath slain . . . They were suborned, Malcolm and Donalbain . . . Are stol'n away . . .** But for a moment there is a monumental calm and dignity in the three phrases of his answer, when Rosse asks him what has been done with the King's body:

Carried to Colmekill,
The Sacred Store-house of his Predecessors,
And Guardian of their Bones.

The narrative of the play takes a step forward, when we hear that Macbeth is already **gone to Scone** to be made King. The trusting Rosse will accompany him thither; but there is an abrupt change in Macduff's tone as he bluntly declares his intention to go home:

No cousin, I'll to Fife.

And there is almost contempt in his mocking twofold echo of Rosse's hesitant **Well . . .**:

Well may you see things well done there.

Since one will to Fife and the other to Scone, Macduff and Rosse leave by opposite Stage-Doors; but before Rosse's departure the Old Man prays he may have the blessing of heaven as his fellow-traveller; and then (left alone with us) extends his prayer for benediction to embrace all men of good will:

God's benison go with you, and with those
That would make good of bad, and Friends of Foes.

He is not speaking ironically; he sees that the only hope in these unnatural times lies in the grace of God and with men like the kindhearted Rosse, who will try to see good even in the wicked. It is a cadence of great beauty, looking forward from the depths of unnatural darkness to the **living Light** of deliverance which ends the play.

*   *   *

[III.i.1–10] After this quiet interlude, Shakespeare loses no time in reviving the tension of his story. The situation is presented now both pictorially and verbally. The curtains of the Study-space part and show us the great thrones for King and Consort, which by their splendour convert the whole Stage into the throne-room. There is good reason to think that the thrones, which are certainly a feature of III.iv (when the Queen 'keeps her State'), are a prominent point of emphasis in this scene too. Banquo's opening words, **Thou hast it now . . .**, the *Senit sounded* of the Folio (a rare direction in Shakespeare, indicating, as always, a formal and extended piece of music for a ceremonial occasion), and the fact that we are seeing Macbeth for the first time, according to the Folio stage-direction, *as King*, all point to the probability of a visible manifestation of 'sovereign sway'; and it is not unlikely that during Macbeth's prolonged and private conversation with Banquo the Queen, as in the later scene, takes her seat on the throne. Moreover the opening line of Macbeth's soliloquy (*line* 48) needs some visible point of reference, some gesture from Burbage, such as striking the arm of the throne on which he is sitting: 'To be *thus*, is nothing. . . .'

Standing and looking up at the thrones is Banquo, who expresses immediately the thought uppermost in his mind, and ours:

> **Thou hast it now, King, Cawdor, Glamis, all,**
> **As the weird Women promis'd . . .**

For the last time the motif of the Witches' triple greeting is sounded, the order in retrospect being reversed, a backward glance over the stages of Macbeth's rise to power. Banquo, whose relationship with Macbeth has been so carefully developed in the first phase of the play, is now the centre of interest. His suspicions are clearly formulated:

> **. . . I fear**
> **Thou play'dst most foully for't.**

But the uncompromisingly honourable stance adopted by him at the discovery of the murder has developed into something more equivocal. We are returned to the Witches' oracular prophecies, that he **should be the Root, and Father Of many Kings**; we remember too his solemn warning to his partner against trusting in the truths told by the instruments of darkness; but now he begins to wonder whether their **truth** may not shine upon him as upon Macbeth: the Weird Sisters (of whom he has dreamt at least once since that meeting on the heath) may be his **Oracles as well**. For the moment silence is the prudent course:

> **But hush, no more.**

[II–47] The entry of the new King, his Lady and his retinue of *Lords, and Attendants*, is an occasion for extravagant splendour. Here and now, visibly before our eyes, Lady Macbeth's dream of 'solely sovereign sway, and Masterdom' has come true. As the formal music of the Sennet comes to a full close, the King, studiedly courteous, at once singles out the waiting Banquo: **Here's our chief Guest**. We are led to expect a coming scene of banquet (it is a regular feature of Shakespeare's stagecraft, this tickling of the curiosity of the audience in anticipation):

> **Tonight we hold a solemn Supper sir,**
> **And I'll request your presence.**

Banquo too is courteous, but his protestation of duty is equivocal: there is a menacing irony in his ambiguous reference to the **most indissoluble tie** which knits him and Macbeth **for ever**. The irony is not lost upon Macbeth: in the urbane exchanges the undercurrent of menace continues. We notice Macbeth's curiosity about Banquo's intended movements. Question and answer lay out for us the blueprint of a sinister and as yet unexpressed design:

> **Ride you this afternoon?**

(for Banquo, the jarring note in the harmony of Macbeth's triumph, even looks incongruous: he is dressed for riding):

> **—Is't far you ride?** ...
> **—I must become a borrower of the Night,**
> **For a dark hour, or twain.**
> **—Fail not our Feast.**

The isolated half-line of Banquo's response has particular emphasis:

> **My Lord, I will not.**

The actor's tone makes the words ponderously memorable. We hear by the way of state matters, the **cruel Parricide** of the young Princes fled to England and to Ireland. But this seems unimportant beside the insistence of the main issue:

**Hie you to Horse:
Adieu, till you return at Night.
Goes Fleance with you?**

The sudden question, unexpected as it is, is peculiarly disquieting. We in the audience cannot fail to understand its secret purpose; for in the soliloquy with which Banquo opened this scene Shakespeare skilfully brought back to our attention the dynastic importance of Fleance. It is not unreasonable to suppose that the boy, booted and cloaked like his father, is present in this scene, receiving the avuncular solicitude of the King's enquiry with an expression of 'absolute Trust'. The court is dismissed with a special reminder of **Supper time**. The order is: **Let every man be master of his time, Till seven at Night**. Then a confidential servant is sent to fetch **those men**, who attend the King's pleasure **without the palace Gate**.

[48–72]   And Macbeth is alone, sitting upon the coveted throne of his ambitions:

To be thus, is nothing.

The dissatisfaction he finds in the achievement of his desire is expressed in his sense of insecurity: he yearns **to be safely thus**. As he speaks of his fear of Banquo, the underlying menace of the preceding dialogue comes closer to the surface. The fact that Banquo has not yet voiced his suspicions openly does not to Macbeth imply connivance: Banquo has a **Royalty of Nature**, he is **dauntless**, but he has too a cautious **Wisdom, that doth guide his Valour, To act in safety**. The comparison to Octavius Caesar[11] is enlightening, for the chilling influence which paralyses Mark Antony may seem to have inhibited Macbeth's energy too: with Banquo out of the way, that energy will break loose in the appalling vigour of Macbeth's last days on earth. One seemingly accidental circumstance of performance on the Globe Stage is that recollection of previous scenes is momentarily evoked through similar placing or a reminiscent posture. So, for instance, on **He chid the Sisters . . .** Burbage rises from his throne and comes forward to the centre of the Stage, reminding us, in movement and gesture, of the very positioning on the Stage of that first meeting with the Witches—the guilty start, the rapt expression, and then Banquo's defiant question and their prophetic answer which **hail'd him Father to a Line of Kings**. It is the neutrality of the Stage during so much of the performance which makes this sort of reminiscence possible. In the anguish of his realisation that he has **fil'd** his mind, destroyed his peace, the language of his soliloquy gathers force, as so often with Shakespeare, in the iteration of motto phrases—**For Banquo's Issue . . . For them . . . Only for them . . . To make them Kings, the Seeds of Banquo Kings**. The loss he has by his own choice suffered (for them) is irrevocable: he has his **eternal Jewel Given to the common Enemy of Man**: he has sold his soul to the devil. He is putting into coherent terms the thought which made him cry 'Wake Duncan with thy knocking: I would thou could'st'. Nevertheless he ends on a note of defiance which we have not heard from him before, but which we might have expected from the ruthless valour of Bellona's bridegroom which was pictured for us in the second scene of the play. Defiant, reckless energy, a mood in which Macbeth seems almost to welcome universal destruction, possesses him more as he heads towards ruin:

> . . . **come Fate into the List,**
> **And champion me to th'utterance.**[12]

[72–142] Although the Folio has the explicit direction *Enter Servant, and two Murtherers*, to us in the audience these new arrivals are not yet identified: they are merely 'those men' who waited outside the palace gate while Macbeth laid bare to us his fear of Banquo. This anonymity of the two men is Shakespeare's deliberate purpose. By the end of the scene they will have *become* murderers: the tension of this leisurely episode lies in the fact that it is a scene of temptation, of seduction to murder (King John, Claudius and Antonio, the usurping Duke of Milan, are among Shakespeare's other practitioners of this subtle art);[13] its detail is not otiose or simply decorative, but instrumental in Shakespeare's dramatic plan; it is through the language itself that the process of temptation is embodied in the action of the play. Macbeth has given his soul to the common enemy of man, and is now about the business of his master, the Devil—the corruption of other men. His dismissal of the Servant (**Now go to the Door, and stay there till we call**) establishes at once the tone of a confidential exchange. The men, shabby as they are in contrast to the King and his brilliant court (we learn soon that they have been beggared by misfortune), are known to Macbeth; only yesterday they were summoned to **conference** with him. The temptation has, in fact, already begun. In Macbeth's recapitulation of their last meeting, we hear that he has exploited their resentment against misfortune: they have been **borne in hand,** oppressed, **cross'd.** And as the rapid verse of his recapitulation comes to its climax, we learn that they have been previously persuaded where the blame for this oppression must lie: **Thus did Banquo.** And so to the **point of second meeting.**

Macbeth renews his temptation with a blasphemy; he sarcastically asks them whether they are so filled with the spirit of charity, as prescribed by the gospels, that they are willing to **pray for this good man** who has ruined them. Richard of Gloster, in many details a cartoon for the portrait of Macbeth, has just such a mockery of the doctrine by which the Christian must counter an incitement to revenge: he professes to meet his friends' encouragement with a demurrer: 'But then I sigh, and with a piece of Scripture, Tell them that God bids us do good for evil.' Macbeth imperceptibly insinuates another thought into the minds of the two men: their resentment is to embrace not only Banquo but also **his Issue** (the very word has its special significance to the audience who have just heard Macbeth's soliloquy). Against his attack on their self-respect, one of his hearers, who are not merely stock figures like the wicked uncles of pantomime, protests with a certain dignity: **We are men, my Liege.** Macbeth takes this touch of pride as the cue for his next attack. What is it to be a man? His theme recalls the weapon used by his Wife against his own indecision (I.vii.47 ff.). The bravura with which he rattles off his **Catalogue** of dogs expresses his contempt for the mongrels who are content to be included in **the Bill, That writes them all alike.** In his implied hierarchy values emerge: against **the slow . . . the Housekeeper . . .** are set in contrast **the swift . . . the subtle . . . the Hunter.** Of such kind are the gifts of **bounteous Nature** which, it seems, will entitle them to a place **not i'th'worst rank of Manhood**. The tone changes from contempt to oblique suggestion: **. . . I will put that Business in your Bosoms . . .** There is a brief insinuation of possible reward (for to do the King's business **grapples you to the heart, and love of us**). And then suddenly the suggestion becomes explicit: nothing short of Banquo's **Death** is in question.

The men both respond to Macbeth's revelation of his purpose, and in their responses there is a nice discrimination of motive. Shakespeare is at pains to give substance even to such minor and anonymous figures. The 'second Murtherer', who has not spoken hitherto, is surly under misfortune and would **spite the World**. His companion grasps at an opportunity to better himself: he would like the chance to **mend** his life, or else **be rid on't**. Their reactions satisfactory so far, Macbeth takes them man to man into his confidence, explains why he may not himself strike openly at Banquo, goes some way even to restore the self-respect he has impugned—**and thence it is, That I to your assistance do make love**. The second murderer will accept unquestioningly Macbeth's command; the other, whose remedy for disastrous life is to kill or cure, begins to blurt out his intention:

Though our Lives— —

The broken dash is a rare example of this punctuation in the Folio: Macbeth cuts short further protestation: **Your Spirits shine through you**. They are men indeed.

It remains to fix the details of their plan—the place, the time, a third party to help them with inside information of Banquo's movements. This is Doctor Johnson's explanation of the obscure line **Acquaint you with the perfect Spy o'th'time**. If he is right, we may paraphrase it thus, 'I will let you know the right moment by means of a fully informed agent' (other editors, however, dispute this interpretation, and suggest that **Spy** is used in a curious sense: 'I will let you know the right moment, determined by careful observation'). There is a feverish energy, reminiscent of Iago and Edmund, in Macbeth's planning:

for't must be done tonight,
And something from the Palace: always thought,
That I require a clearness . . .

Fleance is to be killed too (Banquo's issue must not escape). Our blood
is chilled by the words which condemn the boy to death: he **must**
embrace the fate Of that dark hour: they echo a prophetic phrase
of Banquo's earlier in the scene, the 'dark hour, or twain' which he
must borrow from the night. The echo, with its sinister access of preg-
nant meaning, is a powerful poetical device, close-weaving the texture
of the play, and throwing a ponderous emphasis on the scene we expect
to follow. When the rogues have gone, unhesitatingly **resolv'd** to
undertake this commission, Macbeth delivers his final couplet sitting
on his throne. The Study-curtains close on him, the plan **concluded**
by which he means henceforth 'to be safely thus':

Banquo, thy Soul's flight,
If it find Heaven, must find it out tonight.

*   *   *

[III.ii] The fulfilment of our expectation, as so often in Shakespeare's dramatic plan, is postponed: this is one way of his to sustain
the tension of his story. When the Chamber-curtains open and we see
Lady Macbeth in her private apartment, we grasp at once the shape of
his strategy. For he must guess that we shall be wondering what part
Macbeth's Wife (dearest partner of greatness) is to play in the continuation of the career of murder which she herself initiated. The
appropriate place for this scene is aloft, in the Chamber: the structure
of the playhouse reflects the structure of the play; Lady Macbeth begins
here her withdrawal (interrupted by a resurgence of her strength
summoned up to meet the crisis of the banquet-scene) from a positive
role in her husband's history. Like the scene of her first appearance in
the play, this scene involves but two actors at a time; its nature is
intimate, private, domestic; and just as the phrase 'under my Battlements' gave a hint of placing for the earlier scene, so the situation at
the end of this scene calls imperatively (as we shall see) for the upper

level of the Tiring-House. We must remember the architectural proportions of the playhouse, which make the upper storey of the Tiring-House on a level with, and at no great distance from, the middle of the three Galleries in the auditorium.

[1–56] Her opening enquiry about Banquo reveals the drift of her thoughts. She sends her *Servant* to Macbeth to beg a **few words** at **his leisure**—a strangely docile request. Then, left alone, she echoes her husband's discontent, but with a difference. Although at first her word **safer** seems to be repeating the terms of his dissatisfaction ('to be safely thus'), he will fight to get what he wants: she is already on the road to weary despair. Before he comes, she informs us of her disillusionment. The voice of the boy-player brings an almost ingenuous resignation to the aphoristic shape of the lines, with their formal rhymes, their echo of 'destroy' and 'destruction', and their eloquent alliteration:

> **Nought's had, all's spent,**
> **Where our desire is got without content:**
> **'Tis safer, to be that which we destroy,**
> **Than by destruction dwell in doubtful joy.**

The ensuing dialogue between man and wife is one of the most poignant passages in the play: it loses nothing, gains rather, by being set in the privacy of the Tiring-House. Since we saw the new King and Queen in their royal state, they have not been together: it seems to her that he has fulfilled his declared intention to **keep alone**, and the **sorriest Fancies** which have come to be his **Companions** make his wife still more uneasy. That recurrent motif which is poetically embodied in the words 'do' and 'deed' has powerful expression here in the helpless resignation of her **what's done, is done**. Again the comma of the Folio seems to reflect Shakespeare's rhythm as remembered in the ear of his actor-editors. In contrast to her weary mood, Macbeth is charged with the restless energy of one who is determined to fight 'to th'utterance'. He voices the tyrant's contemptuous disregard for the common good in an image of extreme hyperbole:

> . . . let the frame of things dis-joint,
> Both the Worlds suffer,
> Ere we will eat our Meal in fear . . .

But even as he speaks of the **terrible Dreams, That shake us Nightly** (the rancours in the vessel of his peace), his energy passes into a vein of envy for his dead victim's peace of mind: the magic of poetry, nowhere more powerful than in this scene, presents us with the inimitable contrasts of rhythm and colour in the passage of un-fulfilled longing which follows. As once before in an evocation of sleep, balm of hurt minds, we feel in the speaker the anguish of a mind without peace. The word 'peace' itself, twice used, in a haunting balance of rhythm and with a delicate play of sense (**Whom we, to gain our peace, have sent to peace**), throws into relief the image of the rack, **the torture of the Mind**, to which it gives place. And, in contrast again to this **restless ecstasy**, comes the quiet epitaph of the old King who once was 'shut up in measureless content':

> **Duncan is in his grave:**
> **After Life's fitful Fever, he sleeps well.**

In this passage both 'restless' and 'fitful' must be understood more literally than is customary in our own time. The first expresses pre-cisely the total absence of repose, the second the continual presence of fits, crises of fever. Shakespeare's images sound hackneyed enough: his coinages have become hackneyed by repeated quotation. It is the penalty of their aptness. But to Burbage and to his audience they were fire-new from the mint. Placed thus in the immediate context of the speech, and in the long-range strategy of the play (for Sleep has its echoes up and down the text), the last slow monosyllables have a weight which belies their simplicity. There are other echoes too. When Lady Macbeth rallies her husband and bids him **be bright and Jovial among your Guests tonight**, we remember the false face of hos-pitality with which, at a former banquet, the host and hostess beguiled their unsuspecting guest and king. Echo and reminiscence knit closely the texture of this most compact of plays.

The thought that Banquo is a dangerous obstacle to their content is uppermost in both their minds: yet neither of them gives explicit utterance to the logical solution of this problem, that he must be murdered. The contrast with the overt planning of Duncan's murder is presented with masterly restraint:

—Thou know'st, that Banquo and his Fleance lives.
—But in them, Nature's Copy's not eterne.

Her hesitance is almost pathetic, when we cast our minds back to the earlier scene and the valour of her tongue in scornful chiding.

The climax of the scene, in Macbeth's last two speeches, shows the full force of the poetic drama in the Elizabethan theatre. Towering on the upper level, Burbage broods over the Stage below and creates (no other word is appropriate) the horrible twilight in which murder most foul is to take place. Another **deed** is to be done. Her diffident question **What's to be done?** is a measure of her new hesitance; his **dearest Chuck** (the endearment is, in its context, incongruously horrible) is to **be innocent of the knowledge** until she can **applaud the deed.** The incantatory magic of Macbeth's invocation of **Night** is hypnotic in its effect upon her, and upon us: the **Cloister'd flight** of the bat, the beetle's **drowsy hums,** the image of **seeling** the young hawk's **tender Eye,** the thickening (as it were curdling) of the light, the **Crow** homing to the **Rooky Wood** (sinister contrast, in reminiscence, to Banquo's 'Temple-haunting Martlet', which made the castle of Inverness to seem a place of hospitable welcome), the drooping of Day's **good things,** and the rousing of **Night's black Agents** ready for their prey—it is not surprising that her lord's ecstasy (reminiscent of other moments of his 'rapt' absorption) causes his wife to marvel at his words. His cadence confirms his resolution to fight *à l'outrance*:

Things bad begun, make strong themselves by ill.

*   *   *

[III.iii.1–23] And immediately, as the Chamber-curtains close on his invocation of the dusk, down below on to the great Stage come forth the night's black agents in the person of Banquo's murderers. Here is a striking example of that narrative continuity which is so characteristic a feature of Shakespeare's playhouse. Moreover another feature, the fact of daylit performance, added greatly to the powerful effect of this scene when it was first produced: like other scenes of violence under cover of darkness, such as Roderigo's attempt upon Cassio's life under Iago's expert direction in the penultimate scene of OTHELLO, or Falstaff's highway robbery on Gad's Hill, it gained paradoxically from the very fact that in the daylit playhouse the audience could see what was happening: out of the need to simulate twilight, arose the minute detail of the action, so skilfully created by the poet's evocative dialogue and the miming of the actors.

Three muffled figures creep out of one of the Doors—the two we know, and a stranger whose presence disconcerts the leader. The parts played by the cut-throats are clearly enough distinguished by the numbering of the Folio text. Number 1, who may be taken as the leader, challenges the stranger (Number 3). Number 2 reassures his partner: this is their royal employer's 'perfect Spy of'th'time'.* The leader clinches the atmosphere and the mood—dusk and terror—initiated by Macbeth in his brooding evocation:

The West yet glimmers with some streaks of Day.
Now spurs the lated Traveller apace,
To gain the timely Inn . . .

The words are not spoken in character—no more than Banquo's lines about the temple-haunting martlet; rather less so, indeed, for it is difficult to imagine a vein of lyrical utterance in this crafty cut-throat, 'tugg'd with Fortune'. But just as Banquo's lines were necessary to create the feeling of evening calm and contentment after a long day's journey, so now the Murderer's words are necessary to establish the gathering twilight and (even more important) the panic terror of it, which is prompted by the idea of the hurrying horseman: it is to be noted that he not only describes the aftermath of sunset, but also

* See *page 96, above.*

prompts our feelings and makes us shiver: we, like the lated traveller, would be glad to be under cover, and hope we shall providentially find an inn round the next bend in the road: the word 'timely' is full of suggestion. It is again the stranger (Number 3) whose ears are first to catch the sound of horses: by the skill of the back-stage men we hear them approach and stop; we hear Banquo dismounting and calling for a light; then, to the consternation of Number 1, the horses are heard going away again into the distance; and it is again the stranger who explains why the **Horses go about**:

> **Almost a mile: but he does usually,**
> **So all men do, from hence to th'Palace Gate**
> **Make it their Walk.**

So too at the Gad's Hill robbery Shakespeare shows a similar ingenuity in avoiding the necessity to bring horses on to the Stage: 'Come Neighbour,' says one of the traveller-victims; 'the boy shall lead our Horses down the hill: We'll walk a-foot a while, and ease our Legs.'

When they see Fleance's *Torch* approaching (as once before, his light contributes to the illusion of darkness), they **stand to't**—Numbers 2 and 3 lurking perhaps one each side of the Door through which their victims will come, Number 1 hiding behind the neighbouring Stage-Post (on our side of it, that is, so that we can see the dagger bared behind his back). Fleance leads his father in, and Banquo is beside the Stage-Post as he looks up to the sky, just as he did before, in the similar entry with his son: **It will be Rain tonight**. As the leader deals his blow, Number 2 strikes the torch from Fleance's hand. The boy takes to his heels, dodging round the farther Stage-Post and out by the far Door. It is dramatically satisfactory that, while his father cries out **Thou may'st revenge**, we can (in the daylit theatre) see clearly the survivor's flight. Meanwhile the cut-throats are groping in the dark which they (and Macbeth) have created: it was a blunder, to **strike out the Light**. They soon discover that there is only one dead: they have **lost Best half** of their **Affair**. Two must lug Banquo's body off-stage: the third picks up the torch, a hat, a riding-crop, and anything else that may remain as evidence of the crime—or rather to clutter up the Stage and seem incongruous in the following scene of banquet: perhaps this need is the simple explanation of the presence of the Third Murderer.

*   *   *

[III.iv.1–32] The sequel is again immediate, and the contrast in itself dramatic. The last of the stealthy figures has hardly disappeared through the Door, when the Study-space is opened again to reveal the great double throne. The *Banquet,* which we have been led to expect, is busily and splendidly *prepar'd* by the same crew of servants whom we saw carrying 'Dishes and Service' for Duncan's entertainment under the direction of their Sewer. Their everyday and domestic attendance in the ensuing scene throws into relief the macabre deportment of their betters. The width and depth of the great Globe Stage, and the distinction of its territorial divisions, are fully employed in Shakespeare's design of this crowded and complex episode. The hub of the action is the host's stool in the middle of the Stage, placed so that its occupant will face the audience, at the head of the banquet-table; remote in the Study-space at the back are the two thrones; on either side of the Stage are those areas beyond the Stage-Posts where at significant moments the central persons of the drama will be detached from the company at the table. The banquet-table is set lengthways on the audience's side of the central Trap-Door, and stools are placed round it, equal numbers on each side, one at the end (opposite the host's stool) so that the occupant will have his back to the audience. Candelabra fixed to the Stage-Posts by the servants, and a large branched candle-stick on the table itself, help to dazzle the eyes of the audience and acclimatise them to hallucination.

The entry of the court is ceremonially splendid. The Queen **keeps her State**; that is to say, she sits aloof on the throne, pronouncing her welcome by proxy and at a distance. His Majesty, on the other hand, is in his most affable form, ready to **mingle with Society**. He draws our attention to the central stool, which is just behind the Trap-Door. This disposition is prescribed in the text: **Both sides are even: here I'll sit i'th'midst.** Then bidding his guests make merry, he moves swiftly over to the area outside one of the Stage-Posts, where he has caught sight of his hired assassin. Animated, though inaudible, merriment at the table (with the servants giving occasional attendance) continues during Macbeth's conversation with the Murderer: only Lady Macbeth observes him and, conspicuous on her lofty and lonely eminence, grows increasingly anxious at his absence from the table. The whispered interchange is full of lively characterisation—first Macbeth's hissed rebuke of the man's carelessness—**There's blood upon thy face**: then the undaunted retort, as he wipes his cheek, **'Tis Banquo's then**; next a sort of jesting gusto in brutality, which we shall notice recurring often in Macbeth's declining days (the gusto here embodied in a poetic device; it is not accident of grammatical solecism that produces the jingle of 'thee' and 'he'), **'Tis better thee without, than he within**. The Cut-throat's hesitation in breaking the news of Fleance's escape is followed by a return of that vein of rapt fantasy which is so prominent in Shakespeare's delineation of Macbeth's character: close to the Stage-Post which hides him from his guests, but detaching himself also from his agent in murder, he speaks directly to us and paints the frustration of his desire for release from doubt. The image of the fit, the crisis of fever, which is a flaw in otherwise 'perfect' health, gains in reminiscence of the preceding scenes. Macbeth would wear his health perfect in the death of Banquo (III.i.108); Duncan sleeps well after the fitful fever of life (III.ii.23):

> **Then comes my Fit again: I had else been perfect;**
> **Whole as the Marble, founded as the Rock,**
> **As broad, and general, as the casing Air:**
> **But now I am cabin'd, cribb'd, confin'd, bound in**
> **To saucy doubts, and fears.**

Sharply contrasted with this is the other's crude jesting answer to the question **But Banquo's safe?**—

> **Ay, my good Lord: safe in a ditch he bides . . .**

And the graphic description of his victim, **twenty trenched gashes on his head**, may owe something to the exaggeration of a bungler trying to make the best of a bad job, but we shall remember the phrase when the Ghost of Banquo shakes his gory locks at his sometime partner.

[32–121] With the Stage-Post in between, we are not worried by the proximity of the guests, who are being large in mirth as they await their host's return to the table. It is Lady Macbeth that we notice towards the end of this secret dialogue, for alone on her raised throne she is concerned about her husband's neglect of his guests, and her anxiety, already visible to us, is expressed in words of mild rebuke. Lenox and Rosse are to be Macbeth's neighbours at the table, and they both courteously rise to their feet: **May't please your Highness sit?** Macbeth's response to Lenox's invitation is not immediate: glancing at the Door through which the assassin has just withdrawn, he speaks with feigned regret of the absence of Banquo. Rosse reiterates the request of Lenox. **The Table's full,** says Macbeth; and suddenly we realise that it is. We cannot know for certain the precise conjuring trick by which Banquo's Ghost appears in Macbeth's place, but it seems likely that the extended arms and substantial sleeves and cloaks of the Thanes, who have risen to beg their host to join them, provided a sufficient curtain to veil the manoeuvring of Lowin out of the Trap-Door: or alternatively the manoeuvre, screened in a similar way, could have taken place a little earlier, while the audience's eyes were drawn away from the table by the dialogue with the First Murderer: we will not notice the presence of Banquo until Macbeth's questions draw our attention to the stool. Simon Forman's famous account suggests that there may not have been any trick at all: 'And as he thus did, standing up to drincke a Carouse to him, the ghoste of Banco came and sate down in his cheier behind him.' But the inattentive Doctor's account is not helpful in such matters of detail.

The contrast between the uneventful courtesy of the Thanes and the momently changing reactions of the King is written into the rhythm of the dialogue:

Rosse.   **Please't your Highness**
            To grace us with your Royal Company?
Macb.   **The Table's full.**

Lenox.	Here is a place reserv'd Sir.
Macb.	Where?
Lenox.	Here my good Lord.
	What is't that moves your Highness?
Macb.	Which of you have done this?
Lords.	What, my good Lord?
Macb.	Thou canst not say I did it ...

Flatter, 107, observes that Lenox's answer must follow immediately upon Macbeth's 'Where?' and that the Folio's short line 'Here my good Lord' indicates the pause while Macbeth reacts to the sight of the Ghost. Although most modern editors print both Lenox's lines as a single pentameter, the Folio's lineation seems to suggest that the metrical flow, already disturbed by Macbeth's brusque interjections, is completely broken when he sees the Ghost; and Macbeth's next line ('Which of you have done this?') is in both rhythm and sense a non-sequitur.

The Folio's stage-direction is uncompromising: *Enter the Ghost of Banquo, and sits in Macbeth's place.* Although, through the medium of the poetic drama, Shakespeare has often invited the mind's eye of the audience to see on his bare Stage what is not there, in this case he has preferred to give us, not an empty chair, nor the mechanical atmospherics of music and light, but a visible figure to embody the menace and triumph of the dead man who is father to a line of kings. We certainly see Banquo later among the apparitions raised by the Witches: and there is no reason to think he was any less substantial than the ghosts of Julius Caesar and King Hamlet. To us, and to Macbeth, appears the horrible spectre of Banquo, dressed as we last saw him— but with twenty trenched gashes on his head. And Shakespeare has deployed this treatment before: just as Queen Gertrude could not see the apparition of her dead husband, which we and her son could see, so now the sensible Thanes and the distraught but practical Queen, looking at what we can see, convince us by their skilful miming that they can see nothing. That we in the audience are sharing Macbeth's hallucination draws us into the same case as himself, involves us in the horror of his condition.

Lady Macbeth intervenes, swooping down from her throne; the sharp imperiousness of the tone is achieved by poetical means; no doubt the boy Edmans was instructed to give force to the initial chiasmus and the precise balanced echo of his riposte to Rosse's line:

—**Gentlemen rise, his Highness is not well.**
—**Sit worthy Friends: my Lord is often thus . . .**

It seems likely that her rating of her husband takes place in the remote secrecy beyond the opposite Stage-Post to that area in which he has talked with the Murderer. We are reminded of the earlier scene when she had occasion to use the valour of her tongue upon his weakness. But now she is alarmed and desperate. She employs again a weapon she has before found successful: **Are you a man?** We hear almost casually in passing that he has told her about the **Air-drawn Dagger**, and we are not surprised to find her contemptuous of his **flaws and starts**. She is still as practical and earth-bound as before: **When all's done You look but on a stool.** But we can see Banquo sitting there and nodding; and then, as Macbeth turns away from him on the words **If Charnel houses, and our Graves must send Those that we bury, back . . .** Lenox and Rosse are on their feet once more, and all the other peers this time—and when Macbeth looks back again, the stool is empty:

If I stand here, I saw him.

Although the Folio records the entries of the Ghost, it does not specify the moments of its departure; but they can be certainly deduced from the text. Macbeth's recovery is slow, and he is allowed eight lines of rapt musing, while his Lady is trying to reassure the puzzled Thanes. No doubt Shakespeare, having startled us by the melodramatic spectacle of the blood-stained victim, wished to give a more atmospheric substance to the apparition: it is not enough for this purpose to shock us; we must be frightened, amazed, bewildered by what we have seen:

The times has been,
That when the Brains were out, the man would die,
And there an end: But now they rise again
With twenty mortal murthers on their crowns,

(this is his elaborate decoration of his man's 'twenty trenched gashes')

And push us from our stools. This is more strange
Than such a murther is.

The return of the Ghost is a masterpiece of stagecraft. We have been taken by surprise at its first appearance, and this surprise can hardly be repeated. Instead, we have an intenser experience: it is the effect upon Macbeth of this second onslaught which is the focus of our attention. We see first the astonishing courage of his recovery, and then the recklessness with which the murderer dares his victim to prove his reality by appearing again, by pushing him once more from his stool. Standing beside the very stool, he lifts the cup, newly full, in a toast and underlines his challenge three times, while all the while the Ghost stands waiting at his elbow:

. . . to our dear Friend Banquo, whom we miss . . .

and again

Would he were here . . .

and again

to all, and him . . .

Realisation and defeat come at the very moment when he raises the cup to his lips: the cup drops from his hand, and he shouts at the Ghost:

Avaunt, and quit my sight . . .

The spectre, whose **bones are marrowless**, whose **blood is cold**, who has **no speculation in those eyes** with which he glares at his murderer (each detail is painted for us, in the method of Shakespeare's playhouse, by Macbeth himself), stalks him slowly and relentlessly. Perhaps the boy Edmans heightens the illusion of the Ghost's invisibility by walking between it and Macbeth, the distraught Queen making her frantic attempt to lull the suspicions of the **good Peers**. The Ghost departs, into the Study perhaps, moving without concealment; we know that he is invisible except to Macbeth, and he too, when he has the courage to look again, finds that there is nothing to see: he is **a man again**, and bids his guests **sit still**. But there is no recovery now, and his wife knows it: indeed he himself is past thinking of concealment; he is astonished that anyone can **behold such sights** without losing **the natural Ruby** of the **Cheeks**, and when Rosse presses him to know **what sights**, Lady Macbeth hurriedly interrupts (too much is betrayed already) and dismisses the company without ceremony. Lenox, who will shortly be summing up the state of affairs with shrewd irony, gives us a foretaste of his acid tongue as he turns back to say

> **Good night, and better health**
> **Attend his Majesty.**

[122–144] Nothing, perhaps, about this highly dramatic scene is so poignantly effective as its end, the aftermath. The banquet is not yet cleared away, and the pair sit down together amid the ruins of the feast—the King and Queen still in their royal robes, reduced to the measure of a couple of desperate criminals, in danger of detection:

> **It will have blood they say: Blood will have Blood . . .**

The time of the night is brought to our notice—the small hours—**Almost at odds with morning, which is which**—when the vitality of man is at its lowest ebb. It is a moment of stillness, persuading us in retrospect that in this single scene we have lived through a long night of crisis. There is a similar moment in OTHELLO in a context where the passage of time is of greater importance: at the end of the episode of the discrediting of Cassio, we are given the sense of a long night by Iago's 'by the mass 'tis Morning; Pleasure, and Action, make the hours seem short'. Now, for an instant, action and time are suspended. He and she seem equally pathetic. But he rouses himself, first in indignation against the recalcitrant Macduff who **denies his person At our great bidding** (and we hear **by the way** of the growth of mistrust in this uneasy court—**There's not a one of them but in his house I keep a Servant Fee'd**); then he resolves to revisit **the weird Sisters**—as King Saul in his desperation sought out the Witch of Endor. Once again we are led to anticipate (**betimes**) a coming scene. He knows it is a desperate course: he is **bent to know By the worst means, the worst**. For his **own good, All causes shall give way.** At this moment of suspended action, the metaphor of wading in blood to a point of no return increases our sense of a new resolution in Macbeth. The agonised self-examination which was the prelude to his decision to murder Duncan is a thing of the past: instead of the horrid image of murder which once unfixed his hair and made his seated heart knock at his ribs, now his head is full of **strange things . . . Which must be acted, ere they may be scann'd.** Lady Macbeth's inert reaction is marked by a line of prophetic pathos:

You lack the season of all Natures, sleep.

Her words have their overtones from the night of Duncan's murder and from Macbeth's nostalgic envy of his victim's repose in the grave. **Come, we'll to sleep,** says her husband; but the comfort he offers her is a witness to the growing hardness of his heart; the strange delusions which afflict him are caused not by remorse but by the fear of a novice in crime:

We are yet but young in deed.

The word 'deed' has accumulated an overwhelming force in the past history of the play. That he can tell his wife, almost with relish, that there are yet more deeds to be done makes a strangely callous contrast with the horror of the scene in which he first tells her that he has 'done the deed'. His resolution finds no echo in her broken will. When next we see her, she will be the helpless prey of walking nightmare, for ever lacking the season of all natures, sleep.

*   *   *

[III.vi] If we accept the generally agreed belief that III.v and the subsequent appearance of Hecate in IV.i are interpolations designed to introduce music and songs for the Witches,* then the brief dialogue between Lenox and an unnamed Lord (III.vi) follows directly after the departure of Macbeth and his Lady from the scene of the banquet. This arrangement has led editors to argue that III.vi has not reached us in the form intended by Shakespeare, and either that it is an interpolation too, or that it was originally placed after the Cauldron-scene (IV.i), and has been moved in some process of cutting or reshaping the play. At the end of the Banquet-scene Macbeth declares that he will go early ('betimes') to see the Witches, and so the meeting in IV.i must seem to take place soon after the banquet in III.iv; yet between these two scenes Lenox and the Lord have had time to discover Macduff's disgrace and flight to England; however, Macbeth himself, despite his use of spies, does not learn of Macduff's flight until the end of IV.i. Certainly this difficulty would be avoided if III.vi were to be placed, as editors suggest, after IV.i, but only at considerable cost: there would be a loss of dramatic irony (as the scenes stand, the audience knows that, even while Macbeth is increasing his over-confidence by planning the murder of Macduff, Macduff himself has fled to England to muster the opposition which will overturn Macbeth); secondly, the rearrangement would spoil the very effective juxtaposition, characteristic of Shakespeare's technical method in his own playhouse, of IV.i and IV.ii; thirdly, at the end of IV.i it is Lenox who brings the news that Macduff is in England, and if III.vi were to follow after this, Shakespeare would not have made him ask the Lord where Macduff 'bestows himself'. Shakespeare's time-schemes will not always bear close and rational investigation, since they are calculated less for realistic than for dramatic purposes.

* See *page 22, above.*

Once again the playwright has used the device of suspending our interest by delay: for we are expecting the 'tomorrow And betimes' when Macbeth proposes to visit the Weird Sisters. Instead, we have a scene of conversation—uneventful in the sense that nothing happens or is likely to happen in it: but our ears are sharpened to catch not only the information imparted by the speakers but also their opinions, whether explicit or hinted at, about the matters they discuss. Such another scene is that between Rosse and the Old Man and Macduff (II.iv), and as in that scene, here too the attitude of one of the speakers is expressed ironically. The scene, though static, is dramatically important, and Shakespeare's narrative line has, as usual, an insistent relevance. After Macbeth's suspicious behaviour at the feast, we need to be told of its effect on the Court, and because of the sequel and climax of the play, we need news of the gathering of opposition—and especially of the attitude of Macduff. The episode of Lenox and the Lord acts as a bridge: the appearance of Banquo's Ghost may be considered, in a sense, to close one sequence in the play's action, one development in Macbeth's career of crime; the meeting with the Witches and the decision to slaughter the family of Macduff begin another sequence, another development; the scene in between the two serves first as an interpretative recapitulation and then as a foretaste of the future.

[1–49] The mechanics by which this scene follows directly after the banquet are simple enough: the relics of the feast—table, candelabra, Macbeth's fallen cup—must first be removed by the servants, whose demeanour of awe-stricken haste is in striking contrast to the matter-of-fact and business-like manner with which they prepared the banquet-hall. When the Study-curtains have closed on their handiwork, Lenox and his companion conduct their conversation on the upper level of the Tiring-House. It is possible that the scene, which is entirely unlocalised, took place upon the empty Stage below: but there are considerations which make the upper level seem more appropriate. Lenox may be supposed to want privacy to deploy further the secret nature of his **former Speeches**: the atmosphere of mistrust one associates with tyranny has already begun to develop in the play; Macbeth, we know, has 'a Servant Fee'd' in every house. In the confined limits of the Chamber the confidential mood of the dialogue will be the more effective. Besides, Lenox's speech is in a sense a recapitulation of the action of the play: from their commanding position on the upper level he and his fellow can pointedly give direction to the items of this recapitulation. As Lenox looks down upon a vacant Stage, we are reminded of the scene of Banquo's murder (**Men must not walk too late**) and the terrified flight of his son: we remember the histrionic grief of Macbeth, and his confession that he killed **in pious rage** the sleeping grooms. The mention of danger to **Duncan's Sons** reminds us of the hurried whispering conference of Malcolm and Donalbain at the time of their father's murder. And when the other Lord speaks of his longing for a return of security, so that **we may again Give to our Tables meat, sleep to our Nights,** the idea of violated sleep is especially associated with the area next to the Chamber, where King Duncan's bed-room was; and on the line **Free from our Feasts, and Banquets bloody knives,** he points to where the banquet has just taken place on the Stage below. It is an incidental but dramatically valuable asset of the unlocalised and unchanging stage-building, that such echoes of reminiscence can be invoked by the glance and gesture of an actor.

The actor of the part of Lenox has already shown some skill in the pointing of irony: he professes to give an account of past history, but there is a prudently sarcastic slant in his apparently straightforward relation:

The gracious Duncan
Was pitied of Macbeth: marry he was dead . . .

The speaker's two-edged tongue makes much of the supposed **monstrous** guilt of Malcolm and Donalbain, and the supposed **rage** (both noble and wise) of the murderer, if the drugged chamberlains had lived to protest their innocence. As Lenox speaks of the possibility that Macbeth might hold Duncan's sons in his power, for a moment the ironical tone vanishes and the intensity of his feeling is expressed, though in a parenthesis, openly:

(As, an't please Heaven, he shall not) . . .

Then his caution reasserts itself:

But peace . . .

Macduff, it seems, is in disgrace for speaking too openly.

The anonymous Lord's reply (straightforward in contrast to the other's veiled irony) gives the first sign of gathering opposition to Macbeth, the first hope that the land will one day be delivered from the oppression of tyranny. It is especially important in the structure of the play, for it reminds us that the tragedy, like that of Hamlet or King Lear, is not merely a personal one, the ruin of a once noble man's fortunes, but that it involves the welfare of a whole kingdom. As Lenox's speech has been a recapitulation of the past, so the Lord's reply charts out the play's future course. We are told of Malcolm's welcome at the English Court, of Macduff's going there too, and of the generous exasperation of the English King, who **prepares for some attempt of War**. It is moreover of deliberate purpose that Shakespeare expresses this gathering of opposition in an accumulation of phrases proclaiming sanctity. It is through verbal emphasis that the poet just at this moment (when Macbeth is 'bent to know By the worst means, the worst') recalls the audience to a consciousness of the power of heaven. The English King is **the most Pious Edward** (the Confessor); he receives Malcolm **with such grace**; Macduff is gone to England **to pray the Holy King**; the liberators will rely upon **him above To ratify the Work**. After the lively thumb-nail sketch of Macbeth's **cloudy Messenger** with his taciturn hint of the dangers of rebellion, the images of sanctity return:

> **Some holy Angel**
> **Fly to the Court of England . . .**
> **. . . that a swift blessing**
> **May soon return . . .**

There is no mistaking the earnestness of the cadence—**I'll send my Prayers with him**—which, together with the mention of Macduff, links the scene in our minds with the parting 'benison' of the Old Man in the similar moment of choric comment.

* * *

[IV.i.1–49] As the two quiet-spoken Lords withdraw from sight on the upper level, we are startled by the interruption of a roll of *Thunder* from the Huts above the Heavens; but we are not surprised when it heralds the appearance of *the three Witches* upon the main Stage. We have been expecting them—'I will tomorrow (And betimes I will) to the weird Sisters'—and the story continues its logical course. Shakespeare is not at pains to define or characterise the venue: the editorial head-notes, 'A Cavern', 'A dark cave', are irrelevant here: the only hint of localisation lies in the Second Witch's words 'Open Locks, whoever knocks'. It is interesting that in Holinshed's account of the bewitching of King Duff, a soldier of the garrison discovers the witches at work in a 'house of the towne'. The fact is that Shakespeare, as often, is more concerned with situation than with locality. He quickly focuses our attention upon the Cauldron, which rises from the central Trap-Door (as can be inferred from the fact that Macbeth later in the scene observes it sinking); it becomes the hub of the action, as in the banquet-scene the King's stool had been, for the episode which follows. The Witches have met for a purpose, summoned by their familiar spirits: the cry of the owl, heard once more from the Tiring-House, gives the cue for action, and sharpens the suspense of expectation:

Harpier cries, 'tis time, 'tis time.

Then follows the ungainly dance, circling the cauldron, and the macabre cookery as each item of the cauldron's **Ingredience** is thrown into the **charmed pot**. Probably the effect of this grotesque scene on its first audience was not very unlike the effect it has now. In the hands of Dick Cowley and two of his fellow-comedians, the mumbo-jumbo of that doggerel refrain—**Double, double, toil and trouble**—must surely have raised laughter then as it does today. And this may well have been Shakespeare's intention, shrewd manipulator of audience-reaction that he was. The list of items, voiced in trochaic incantation, begins by being more disgusting than sinister: the **poison'd Entrails**, the **swelt'red Venom** of the sleepy **Toad**, the **Fillet of a Fenny Snake . . . Eye of Newt, and Toe of Frog**—each poisonous item conjured up in visible imitation or by inventive gesture (as, for instance, a fluttering gesture of hovering descent which gives substance to the **Howlet's wing**)—these are loathsome, as we imagine them to **boil and bake** in the cauldron. It is a strange fact of human nature that the public declamation of loathsome and revolting detail provokes laughter, a sort of compensating reaction to disgust. But when laughter has lowered our guard, we become suddenly vulnerable to a keener thrust: and for this purpose Shakespeare has made the third Sister sound a more sinister note; her incantation, including the Jew, the Turk, the Tartar, and the victim of infanticide, brings us nearer to the dangerous wickedness of black magic:

> **Liver of Blaspheming Jew . . .**
> **Nose of Turk, and Tartar's lips:**
> **Finger of Birth-strangled Babe,**
> **Ditch-deliver'd by a Drab . . .**

For Shakespeare's audience, each of these creatures, lacking the grace of baptism, adds to the sense that this concoction is a work of evil. The poet, we may be sure, urged his Witches to take themselves seriously, however much their appearance and demeanour and words made the audience laugh. Gradually the intensity of their concentration on their gruesome task freezes the smile on our face and chills our blood. Our early laughter in no way diminishes the tragic fact that these contemptible crones have power over Macbeth and that he is prepared to put his faith in them. With the King's entry the scene takes on a tone as sinister and dangerous as that of King Saul's visit to Endor. The preparation of the bubbling cauldron has become

A deed without a name.

[50–124] And Macbeth himself, in his conjuration, heightens their stature as 'Instruments of Darkness'. He is 'bent to know By the worst means, the worst'; for his own good 'All causes shall give way': and his repeated demand of **answer me . . .** frames a mounting climax of devastation which may be the price of his dabbling with the occult:

> **though the treasure**
> **Of Nature's Germens tumble all together,**
> **Even till destruction sicken: Answer me**
> **To what I ask you.**

Even so Lear invokes universal destruction, bidding the thunder to 'Crack Nature's moulds, all germens spill at once That makes ingrateful Man' (KING LEAR, III.ii.8 f.). In the event, Macbeth's question is not voiced: he will **hear it**—whatever it is—from their **Masters**. That the Apparitions rose from the cauldron, already located over the Trap-Door, can be inferred from the stage-directions of the Folio—*He Descends . . . Descends . . . Descend*. A busy afternoon for the mechanics in the cellarage. And when the first Apparition rises, *an Armed Head*, out of the steaming cauldron, Macbeth's attempted enquiry is interrupted by the first Witch:

> **He knows thy thought:**
> **Hear his speech, but say thou nought.**

To **beware Macduff**, that was indeed his thought.

> **—   But one word more.**
> **—He will not be commanded.**

Again before the question is explicit, the Apparition is succeeded by a second, **more potent than the first**: one of the Witches lifts from the cauldron a naked infant, blood-stained from a Caesarian birth, and rocks it with clumsy dandling in the crook of her arms. The baby whimpers his name three times, and Macbeth's mocking **Had I three ears . . .** is the reckless jest of a man who knows that his soul is in danger of damnation. He cannot read the riddle, **none of woman born Shall harm Macbeth**. Macduff shall live—yet no, he shall not: Macbeth yearns to be rid of his fears, and **sleep in spite of Thunder**.

Thunder has heralded each Apparition in turn, and now the third rises from the cauldron, even more puzzling than the last—*a Childe Crowned, with a Tree in his hand*; from him comes an invitation to pride, courage, and unflawed confidence, at least until the impossible miracle of a moving forest. **Sweet bodements, good,** says Macbeth, and the sequel shows how much store he sets upon their encouragement.

The significance of the three Apparitions has been variously explained, but it seems likely that each Apparition symbolises one of the stages in Macbeth's downfall, and refers to it in his utterance. The first Apparition, then, represents the head of Macbeth himself, to be severed by Macduff at the end of the play; the first Witch's warning ('he knows thy thought') is, therefore, grimly ironical. The head is raised on a pole or pike from the cauldron and the severed neck is stained with blood: the same gruesome property head will reappear in the last scene of the last Act. The second Apparition, *a Bloody Childe*, represents Macduff who 'was from his Mother's womb Untimely ripp'd' (V.vii.44 f.). The third Apparition represents Malcolm who marches against Macbeth, his army concealed by the leafy boughs of Birnam Wood. By an appropriately devilish ambiguity the Crowned Child may also suggest the children of Banquo who are to succeed to the Scottish throne; the tree which admits of a more literal interpretation in the equivocal prophecy about Birnam Wood, may have suggested to the first audience the family tree of the Stuarts (of whom Banquo was 'Root, and Father'). Possibly Shakespeare had in mind the illustration in Bishop Leslie's *De Origine*.[14]

Macbeth's misguided confidence is eloquently expressed in the verbal shape of his reaction to the third Apparition's prophecy. Picking up the half-line with which it ends, he continues in rhyming couplets, which catch the lilt of the Crowned Child's oracular verse. It is not till the uneasiness of his heart, which **throbs to know one thing,** provokes a further question, that his rhyme-scheme breaks down: and now the question is at last explicit:

**Shall Banquo's issue ever
Reign in this Kingdom?**

The Weird Sisters utter an urgent, sinister warning:

Seek to know no more.

As he insists, with threats of **an eternal Curse**, music of *Hoboyes* sounds from the recesses of the Tiring-House, and the cauldron sinks before his eyes. It has been the centre of dramatic interest since the beginning of the scene, but now our attention is drawn elsewhere, as the Study-curtains open and the Weird Sisters solemnly present their Dumb Show:

Show his Eyes, and grieve his Heart,
Come like shadows, so depart.

The opening of the Study-curtains at this point reinforces the suggestion, implicit in the words of the Witches, that the 'show' is a kind of dramatic spectacle performed for Macbeth. It is interesting that the word 'shadow', used so often to indicate the unreal and impermanent, is a favourite image for the actor who represents real life (as in V.v. 24 ff., and A MIDSUMMER NIGHT'S DREAM, V.i.215, V.ii.54). *A shew of eight Kings, and Banquo last, with a glasse in his hand.* Macbeth's speech indicates clearly the form the procession should take, but it is inconsistent with the stage-direction of the Folio, by which the figure who bears the glass should be Banquo himself: Macbeth's words show that it is the eighth king who bears the glass, and that Banquo follows him to claim them all as his descendants. Burbage fits Shakespeare's words with the passage of the individual kings: the text makes quite clear the moment when each of the eight is momentarily the central figure: the hired men of the company were no doubt rigorously drilled in the pace and spacing of their procession. **What, will the Line stretch out to th'crack of Doom?** is Macbeth's reaction to the fifth king: **Another yet?** greets the sixth. Macbeth, who has retreated in revulsion from the seventh king, finds himself drawn hypnotically towards the **glass** borne by the eighth; it is not a mirror, but the crystal ball traditionally used for divination, like the 'glassie globe' devised by Merlin for King Ryence in *The Faerie Queene* (Book III, Canto II, 21).

Macbeth studies the globe closely to make out the **two-fold Balls, and treble Sceptres** of the united kingdoms.[15] At the end of the series comes Banquo, still **Blood-bolter'd** with the gashes on his head, and claims with a smile of vindictive triumph this royal progeny **for his.**

[133–156] If we reject the grotesque dancing of the Witches (to cheer up Macbeth's spirits) as of a piece with the interpolation of the Hecate-scenes,* we must suppose that Burbage, at sight of the triumphant Banquo, hides his face, and when he looks again, both Dumb Show and Witches have disappeared by the closing of the Study-curtains. As he stands alone upon the bare and empty Stage, crying **Where are they? Gone?** we shall find ourselves wondering, with him, if the whole encounter with the Witches has been an illusion (as Banquo said at an earlier meeting, 'Were such things here, as we do speak about? Or have we eaten on the insane Root, That takes the Reason Prisoner?'). At the same time the sound of horses approaching at a gallop and coming to a halt is heard outside the Door by which Macbeth entered the Stage. These are the **two or three . . . that bring you word: Macduff is fled to England.** Lenox enters by this Door, summoned from where he was waiting **without there.**

—Saw you the Weird Sisters?
—No my Lord.
—Came they not by you?
—No indeed my Lord.

The note of sceptical irony, which we have learnt to associate with Lenox's character, sounds again in his answers to Macbeth's questioning: it is the tone of the sane man humouring the lunatic. The news that Macduff has **fled to England**—the words repeated with the furious intensity of a thunderclap—carries Burbage to the front of the Stage, out of the hearing of Lenox: in the violent determination of the ensuing speech we see again the growing hardness of Macbeth's heart. Now the **deed** must not wait upon **the flighty purpose:**

* See *page 22, above.*

**From this moment,
The very firstlings of my heart shall be
The firstlings of my hand.**

The savage energy of his murderous plan to surprise Macduff's castle
(**be it thought and done**) is hurled at the groundlings immediately
below him. Contrasted with this energy is the growling murmur of

But no more sights.

We have heard this word 'sights' before (III.iv.114 ff.): the phrase
includes in its irritable disgust not only the apparitions of the cauldron
and the procession of Banquo's issue but the blood-boltered Banquo
himself shaking his gory locks over the festal board of his murderer's
solemn supper. It is significant that from this point, when Macbeth
finally thrusts away the hesitations of conscience and remorse, he is
never again troubled by supernatural visions or the pictures of his
tormenting imagination. King James I, in the *Basilikon Doron*, published
in England in 1603, described perceptively the action of conscience
after a man has turned to wickedness: first, chastised by his conscience,
he will fall into superstition, as Macbeth turned to the powers of darkness; and finally, his conscience 'cauterized', he will become 'senselesse
of sin'. Macbeth's conscience has become fully cauterized.

*   *   *

[IV.ii.1–83]   The course of Shakespeare's narrative is often emphasised in the stage-directions of the Folio: so now, after we have heard
of Macbeth's intention to surprise the castle of Macduff and 'give to
th'edge o'th'Sword His Wife, his Babes . . .', we read, as an immediate
sequel, *Enter Macduffes Wife, her Son, and Rosse*. It is with a shudder
that we see the family group (Rosse, we remember, is a cousin of the
family) in the domestic surroundings of the Chamber. The effect of
this sequence of scenes, powerful in the dramatist's deployment of
contrasting atmosphere and ironical juxtaposition, relies for its success
on the swift continuity made possible by scene-distribution on the
multiple stage. Shakespeare's problem (if we express it mechanically)

is to give enough substance to Macbeth's innocent victims before he shows their murder. Once again he has made a virtue of necessity: he has used the opportunity, to begin the elaboration of Macduff's role which is a necessary part of the structure of the play. And he has chosen an ingenious method to achieve his purpose, a method which is characteristic of his poetic drama: he has focused our interest upon a single topic, the theme of treachery; and he has done this by verbal repetition; the word 'traitor' is prominent at the beginning of the scene, it is the subject of the young boy's questioning, and it makes a resounding climax at the moment of the murderer's assault. In the process, he has given lively if brief characterisation to both mother and son, and made Macduff's bereavement the more poignant for us.

Lady Macduff is not at all the sweet helpless innocent: she is indignant and resentful at her husband's departure, and hardly stops short of calling him a coward, to leave his family **in a place From whence himself does fly**. Rosse has already had an opportunity, in the quiet aftermath of Duncan's murder, to deploy his pleasant character of ineffectual good-will. Then he was at a loss to understand how Malcolm and Donalbain could want to murder their father, and was puzzled rather than enlightened by the clear-sighted irony of his cousin Macduff. Now he is hoping against all reason for the best: he knows his cousin to be **Noble, Wise, Judicious**; he expresses the helplessness of a good man perplexed in evil times. Fastening upon the Lady's protest that **our fears do make us Traitors**, he presents the agonising dilemma with which tyranny confronts patriots:

> **. . . cruel are the times, when we are Traitors**
> **And do not know our selves.**

Macduff's love for Scotland has sent him to England, but it has also made him, without his realising it, a traitor to his family. The actor (Baldwin ascribes the part of Rosse to Heminges) makes it clear that Rosse is speaking not only of Macduff, but also of himself: a good-hearted man, he has given his allegiance to Macbeth for the best of reasons (to 'make good of bad'), and is only now coming to realise that this makes him a traitor to the true interests of Scotland. When we next see him, he will have joined the opposition in England. As he says **Shall not be long but I'll be here again**, we (who have heard Macbeth's purpose) feel sick at heart with apprehension: as he adds his conviction that **Things at the worst will cease, or else climb upward, To what they were before**, we feel that here is poor comfort for this defenceless family. That he himself lacks faith in his own words is clear from the tears that stand in his eyes as he asks a **Blessing** upon the little boy. Ashamed of betraying his emotion, he takes his **leave at once**. We shall remember these tears when it falls to his lot to break the news of bereavement to Macduff; and again we shall be conscious of the warm heart of the man, when in the last scene of the play he has to tell another father of the death of his son in battle.

The boy's portrait is no more perfunctorily conventional than his mother's: he is indeed full of life and character, like those other children whose particular brand of spirited vitality gives an edge to pathos, Prince Arthur in KING JOHN, Mamillius, Leontes's sprightly son in THE WINTER'S TALE, and Coriolanus's boy—a pugnacious chip of the old block. Young Macduff has been busy at play or reading a book while his elders talk, but we notice that he lifts his head for an instant, cocking one ear as his mother utters the word **Traitors**. When, after Rosse's departure, she speaks to him, his first answers seem thrown off, with half his attention still on his game or his book: and the wit of **Poor Birds they are not set for** betrays, with its sardonically emphasised adjective, a little irritation at her term of endearment. **My Father is not dead for all your saying** has the unexpected abruptness of real conversation, and there is more than a pert retort in the shrewd counter-question: **Nay how will you do for a Husband?** He is calling her bluff. Certainly he abandons his occupation when he confronts her with the question which has been turning in his mind since the opening of the scene: **was my Father a Traitor, Mother?** The dictum that a traitor is **one that swears, and lies** had its obvious topical reference (in the ears of the play's first audience) to the equivocation of the Jesuit Father Garnet: and the boy's ingenious exercise in logic, with its triumphant conclusion **Then the Liars and Swearers**

are Fools . . ., makes his mother (and us) laugh, and turns the theme of traitors and hanging to comedy for the moment. But in the context of the scene, with its previous discussion of the theme of traitors, the talk of the **poor prattler** is centrally relevant. When Lady Macduff reverts to his father's supposed death, he calls her bluff again: **If he were dead, you'ld weep for him: if you would not, it were a good sign, that I should quickly have a new Father.** Then, content with his dialectical victory, he returns to his previous occupation, remaining quite unaware that a stranger has appeared, unaware too of this **homely man's** warning of imminent danger. The messenger's apology (**Methinks I am too savage**) implies already some alarm from Lady Macduff; but this child, whom the playwright has portrayed as so spirited and quick-witted, is silent both now and during his mother's subsequent words of alarm: we must suppose that he remains absorbed in his own concerns.

The climax is masterly. At the entry of the assassins, the Lady, embodying her own earlier image of **the poor Wren (The most diminutive of Birds)** who **will fight, Her young ones in her Nest, against the Owl**, discards at once her indignation at her husband's flight, and defies them with aristocratic contempt, echoing in her negative description of his refuge the impression of sanctity we already associate with England:

> —Where is your Husband?
> —I hope in no place so unsanctified,
>   Where such as thou may'st find him.

We are not spared the horror of murder most foul, but the boy's heroism makes the heart beat faster, and there is a poetic rightness in the fact that it is called forth by that same accusation which he has questioned in playful argument before:

> —He's a Traitor.
> —Thou li'st thou shag-ear'd Villain.

His dying words are concerned with his mother's safety, and we hear her screams (*Exit crying Murther*) as she runs into the distance, pursued by the cut-throats. The Chamber-curtains close on the abrupt silence which tells us that she too is dead.

*   *   *

[IV.iii.1–139]   The mere appearance of Malcolm and Macduff on the Stage below informs us that the scene is now transported to the English Court, which has so recently been invested with sanctity by the words of Lenox and his companion. Once again both the swift continuity and the effect of ironical contrast in this sequence are strengthened by the distribution of scenes on the multiple stage. Malcolm's opening words prepare us—both by their relaxation of rhythm (a striking contrast with the violent ending of the preceding episode) and by their quietist sentiment—for a long and leisurely conversation:

> **Let us seek out some desolate shade, and there**
> **Weep our sad bosoms empty.**

A tension of personalities is already in evidence in Macduff's retort to this self-indulgent inactivity, his robust exhortation to **bestride our downfall'n Birthdom**. With the echo of his wife's cries still ringing in our ears, the tragic irony of his description of Scotland's plight is sharply apparent in the iterance of

> **Each new Morn,**
> **New Widows howl, new Orphans cry . . .**

and the ironical point is driven home in Malcolm's subsequent words, **He hath not touch'd you yet.** Clearly the conflict of attitude between the two is to be fought out against the background of a tragic development of which neither is yet aware.

The scene which follows is the longest in the play and, during its long deployment, Shakespeare makes no use of violent action or sensational incident, to hold the attention of the audience. This is not to say that the scene is undramatic, or that Shakespeare's stagecraft flags at this point. The tension has been kept taut almost continuously since the beginning of the play: now it is deliberately relaxed, both to give some necessary relief to the strained senses of the audience, and also to show us that Macbeth's tyranny is but a nightmare, and that there is a world of wholesome reality elsewhere. For the long duologue between Malcolm and Macduff Shakespeare is following Holinshed very closely: the interest is sustained in the slow resolution of our uncertainty. Of Malcolm we have been shown in earlier scenes only enough to excite our curiosity; and his character is a crucial matter of public importance, if he is to head the opposition against the tyrant. Our acquaintance with Macduff too is growing; his introduction into the play was long delayed and he has appeared but briefly hitherto, but our eagerness to know more of him has increased through what we have heard of his public behaviour and what we have seen of his private fortunes. His abrupt decision to absent himself from Macbeth's coronation, his refusal to answer the King's summons, his 'broad words' and the failure of 'his presence at the Tyrant's Feast', the news given to Lenox that he has gone to join Malcolm at the English Court, and the solemn warning of the first Apparition to 'Beware the Thane of Fife', are all judiciously placed sign-posts on Shakespeare's path to the establishment of Macduff as the main hope of Scotland's salvation. Then the path seems suddenly blocked by two disconcerting questions —the first with an implication of censure, 'What had he done, to make him fly the Land?'; the second artlessly frank, '*Was* my Father a Traitor, Mother?' Drama is created out of unresolved discords, and there is a double tension in this conversation: Malcolm is suspicious of Macduff, in case he should prove to be one of Macbeth's agents; Macduff, all eager to support Malcolm in an attempt to rescue his country from the tyrant's grasp, finds himself confronted with an unexpected obstacle to his hopes. On the one hand is, it seems, pusillanimous caution, and on the other, unthinking rashness. This mutual tension Shakespeare has developed at large, adding his own eloquence of rhythm and vocabulary to the spare debate reported at length in his source.

Malcolm's prudent response to the older man's positive passion is portrayed in the hesitant phrases of tentative probing—

> you have lov'd him well,
> He hath not touch'd you yet. I am young, but something
> You may deserve[16] of him through me, and wisdom
> To offer up a weak, poor innocent Lamb
> T'appease an angry God . . .

and again in swift rejoinder—

> —I am not treacherous.
> —But Macbeth is . . .

and again in sudden direct enquiry—

> Why in that rawness left you Wife, and Child?
> Those precious Motives, those strong knots of Love,
> Without leave-taking.

The question makes Macduff wince, and the suspicion that prompts it drives him to an impulsive feint of despair:

> Fare thee well Lord,
> I would not be the Villain that thou think'st,
> For the whole Space that's in the Tyrant's Grasp,
> And the rich East to boot.

This draws from Malcolm a concession to the other's manifest sincerity:

> Be not offended:
> I speak not as in absolute fear of you . . .

But then he embarks on a deliberate stratagem, designed to deceive Macduff and no doubt, in Condell's interpretation of the scene, his audience as well. It is, of course, possible that the actor stood on the perimeter close to the groundlings, and took them with a sly glance (Falstaff-wise) into his confidence. But it seems more probable that

Shakespeare's instruction was to play his trick of deception with a poker-face. We too are dismayed to hear that, if the tyrant is overthrown in the coming struggle, the **poor Country** is likely to suffer more **by him that shall succeed**. It is no accident but Shakespeare's deliberate intention that the difference of attitude between the two is now expressed in a discussion of ethics. Malcolm's testing of Macduff has changed its direction: he is no longer concerned with his honesty but with his values: at what moral cost will he accept the kingship of Malcolm? This testing of Macduff becomes a kind of dialectic in which the values of the play are worked out and affirmed. In himself, so the young man to our astonishment declares, **all the particulars of Vice** are **so grafted** that in comparison **black Macbeth Will seem as pure as Snow**. He dilates with a kind of morbid relish on the insatiable appetite of his **Voluptuousness**. Macduff so far stifles his instinctive dislike as to suggest that a lecherous king may take his pleasures in secret—

> **you may**
> **Convey your pleasures in a spacious plenty,**
> **And yet seem cold. The time you may so hoodwink:**
> **We have willing Dames enough . . .**

So he tops one vice with another, **stanchless Avarice**. This admission is greeted with a growl from the thrifty Scottish Thane: **This Avarice sticks deeper** (*Radix malorum est cupiditas*):

> **yet do not fear,**
> **Scotland hath Foisons, to fill up your will**
> **Of your mere Own. All these are portable,**
> **With other Graces weigh'd.**

But I have none, cries Malcolm, and so brings his confession to a head with a recital of **the King-becoming Graces** which he lacks:

> **As Justice, Verity, Temp'rance, Stableness,**
> **Bounty, Perseverance, Mercy, Lowliness,**
> **Devotion, Patience, Courage, Fortitude . . .**

His diatribe ends in cosmic hyperbole:

> Nay, had I pow'r, I should
> Pour the sweet Milk of Concord, into Hell,
> Uproar the universal peace, confound
> All unity on earth.

'Concord' and 'universal peace' were themes dear to King James's heart, and the rhetorical climax owes its origin perhaps to the poet's desire of pleasing his royal patron.[17] But the emphasis on the 'King-becoming Graces' at this point in the play—sharply contrasted with the recent recital of Macbeth's vices (**I grant him Bloody, Luxurious, Avaricious, False, Deceitful, Sudden, Malicious, smacking of every sin That has a name**)—is structurally important. It enlarges the field of the tragedy, lifts it from the personal to the national plane, and from the national to the universal; and it reminds us of that theme which is never far from Shakespeare's thought in his historical studies, the dependence of the people for their happiness upon the person, the conduct and the character of their King. The wickedness of Macbeth (and the supposed wickedness of his likely successor) is Scotland's tragedy, and there is the nobility of statesmanship in Macduff's great outcry:

> O Scotland, Scotland.
> . . . O Nation miserable!
> With an untitled Tyrant, bloody Sceptr'd,
> When shalt thou see thy wholesome days again?

The word 'wholesome' initiates the imagery of sickness and health which will pervade the last movement of the play. Macduff's retrospective picture of Malcolm's parents strikes once more the note of sanctity, which bestows on the future rebellion the character of a crusade:

> Thy Royal Father
> Was a most Sainted-King: the Queen that bore thee,
> Oft'ner upon her knees, than on her feet,
> Di'd every day she liv'd.

Malcolm's volte-face is the more effective, since it takes us by surprise: the contrast between his lurid description of imaginary vices and the simplicity of his recantation is itself dramatic. He reveals the reason for his elaborate deception:

> **Devilish Macbeth,**
> **By many of these trains, hath sought to win me**
> **Into his power: and modest Wisdom plucks me**
> **From over-credulous haste . . .**

And as we hear him **unspeak** his **own detraction,** we cannot fail to be touched by the half-humorous confession that

> **My first false speaking**
> **Was this upon myself.**

Most convincing is Shakespeare's portrayal of the reaction of Macduff; no immediate enthusiasm, but a bewildered silence:

> **Such welcome, and unwelcome things at once**
> **'Tis hard to reconcile.**

[140–159] In Macduff's hesitation the tension is still unresolved: the process of resolution begins in the strange little episode which follows—the passing by of the English Doctor on his way to see the King bestowing **his touch** upon **a crew of wretched Souls That stay his Cure,** and the subsequent portrait of King Edward which Malcolm gives in answer to Macduff's question. The passage has been considered to be merely a contemporary compliment to King James, or a topical commentary on the ceremony of the Royal Touch, and James's attitude to it. It is, however, more than that, and has its dramatic purpose in the structure of Shakespeare's play. We have already heard, in the words of Lenox's anonymous companion, how the imagery of sanctity gives a special character to the court of the Confessor. This effect is now reinforced by the Doctor's description of how

THE TRAGEDY OF MACBETH

> at his touch,
> Such sanctity hath Heaven given his hand,
> They presently amend.

And Malcolm's graphic portrait, spoken in a theatre where the audience were used to seeing pictures with the mind's eye, makes **this good King** (although he never appears) a living personality, a present force for good, in the course of Shakespeare's narrative:

> how he solicits heaven
> Himself best knows: but strangely visited people
> All swoln and Ulcerous, pitiful to the eye,
> The mere despair of Surgery, he cures,
> Hanging a golden stamp about their necks,
> Put on with holy Prayers.

A King who possesses the power of **healing Benediction** is the best ally for those whose urgent mission is to restore 'wholesome days' to their sick country. Just as in this episode the image of sickness is given palpable embodiment, so too are the images of holiness: Lady Macduff in her courageous answer to the murderer hoped that her husband was 'in no place so unsanctified Where such as thou may'st find him': now in England that husband hears of the **sanctity** of the good King and the **sundry Blessings** that **hang about his Throne.**

[160–239] With the entry of Rosse the intensity of the play is at once revived. We know why he has come: we have seen the murder of Macduff's family: our expectation hangs upon the moment when the news will be broken. Shakespeare does not hurry the coming of that moment: he knows well how to profit by the interval of suspense. At first Malcolm does not recognise the newcomer; manifestly, by his dress, a fellow-**Countryman**, he may be another of the tyrant's spies: then Macduff's affectionate welcome (confirming our previous impression of that **ever gentle Cousin**) reassures Malcolm, and he prays that the time will soon come when friends need no longer be **Strangers.** In Rosse's description of the state of Scotland, Shakespeare's

power of crystallising common experience in memorable phrase is at
its height:

> **where nothing**
> **But who knows nothing, is once seen to smile . . .**

The phrase (with its ear-catching verbal pattern) evokes an easily re-
cognisable distinction between apathy and involvement; the contrast
of **violent sorrow** with **Modern ecstasy** is not only in sense but in
the syllabic chiasmus of its sound; and the compression of much
thought and feeling in little compass—

> **the Deadman's knell**
> **Is there scarce ask'd for who . . .**

matches in density the poet's near contemporary, John Donne. With
startling abruptness, Macduff asks him point-blank for news of his
family:

> **—How does my Wife?**
> **—Why well.**
> **—And all my Children?**
> **—Well too.**
> **—The Tyrant has not batter'd at their peace?**
> **—No, they were well at peace, when I did leave 'em.**

The repetition gains in pathos from a verbal echo: Duncan, we remember, in Macbeth's phrase, was 'sent to peace', and now 'sleeps
well' (III.ii.20, 23). The iteration of the euphemisms 'well' and 'peace'
(familiar from the irony of Greek tragedy) is not merely a perfunctory
trick of the dramatist: it is a poignant expression of this gentle cousin's
reluctance to **transport the Tidings** which he has **heavily borne**.
There is something altogether life-like about the way in which he
turns for the moment away from Macduff to Malcolm, using the tone
of exhortation:

> **Now is the time of help: your eye in Scotland**
> **Would create Soldiers . . .**

In Malcolm's reassuring reply we hear (not for the first time) of **good Siward** who is to lead the English force:

> **An older, and a better Soldier, none**
> **That Christendom gives out.**

But the news must be broken, and by hints and forewarnings Rosse leads his cousin to the brink of discovery.

The news when it comes is given bleakly—the facts without description. Rosse, the ever gentle cousin, will not **relate the manner** of the savage slaughter. His compassionate reticence and Macduff's speechless agony are skilfully thrown into relief against the too facile exhortation of the young Prince: moreover Shakespeare uses Malcolm's outburst (in the method of the poetic drama in the Jacobean playhouse) to portray and interpret Macduff's bereavement. He learnt some years ago, in handling the bereavement of Brutus, how to render in terms of verbal expression the restrained silence of the 'o'er-fraught heart'. Macduff's grief is at first wordless:

> **What man, ne'er pull your hat upon your brows:**
> **Give sorrow words; the grief that does not speak,**
> **Whispers the o'er-fraught heart, and bids it break.**

The metaphor of **Med'cines ... To cure this deadly grief** continues the imagery of health and sickness initiated earlier in the scene. It is tempting to see a rebuke to Malcolm in the words **He has no Children.** Most actors, perhaps, will prefer the more obvious application to Macbeth. King James's Men, having the author to tell them what he meant, would have been in no doubt. Certainly it is Malcolm's callow insistence that looses the bereaved man's tongue at last, and it is worth noting the technical means by which Shakespeare emphasises this point. Macduff's urgent questions to the now silent Rosse end (in the precise and vividly pictorial metaphor of the kite's raid upon the farmyard) with a half-line:

**What, All my pretty Chickens, and their Dam
At one fell swoop?**

Malcolm's tactless exhortation completes the line:

Dispute it like a man.

Whereupon Macduff, resenting the implication of weakness, completes Malcolm's half-line:

**—Dispute it like a man.
—I shall do so:
But I must also feel it as a man . . .**

Such a subtle manipulation of verse-lengths is not obscured by the Folio's habit of printing each speech close to the speech-heading. For a moment Macduff's condemnation turns upon himself:

**Sinful Macduff,
They were all struck for thee: Naught that I am,
Not for their own demerits, but for mine
Fell slaughter on their souls . . .**

And we share the pain of his remorse, as we remember his wife's unanswered question—'Wisdom? to leave his wife . . . ?' But then Malcolm's persuasion—**Be this the Whetstone of your sword**—converts his grief to anger, and his challenge to **this Fiend of Scotland** anticipates in prospect the final confrontation of the play:

**Within my Sword's length set him, if he 'scape
Heaven forgive him too.**

The scene ends on a note of stirring determination: **Come go we to the King** recalls the exasperation of the 'most Pious Edward' which has prompted him to prepare 'for some attempt of War', and gains extra weight from the brief episode of the English Doctor and the Royal Touch. We may think of Malcolm's enthusiasm as having some of the insensitive tactlessness of youth, but we cannot help applauding the change (**This tune goes manly**) from the mood of the scene's opening speech. Malcolm and Macduff have tested each other, and the ultimate touchstone has been that private grief in which 'no mind that's honest but . . . shares some woe'. Malcolm's new manliness has shown him fit to succeed to his father's throne: Macduff meanwhile has grown to the stature of a protagonist. There is a special interest in the possibility, if we follow Baldwin, that two of the players in the moving climax of this scene were the editors of the First Folio: Heminges as Rosse and Condell as Malcolm would, we may suppose, have felt a touch of nostalgia in the handling of this particular page of their fellow-actor's prompt-book.

The Christian values of the play are affirmed. The last lines of the scene strongly communicate the sense of a turning-point: first there is an invocation of **the Powers above**; it is not only revenge, but a sense of mission, as **Instruments** of those powers, that will give strength of purpose to Malcolm, Macduff and Siward (whose name as a soldier rings through Christendom). And finally the unnatural darkness which on the morrow of Duncan's murder did 'the face of Earth entomb' begins to lift: there will be 'living Light' again:

The Night is long, that never finds the Day.

*   *   *

[V.i.1–86] The last movement of the play begins here. It is masterly in the simplicity of its structure. The battle-sequence, which so often occupies Shakespeare's last Act and should contain the climax of the action, appears usually in modern performance as a shapeless, incoherent anti-climax. Several of the historical plays (for instance, KING JOHN, 1 HENRY IV, JULIUS CAESAR) seem to peter out in an unintelligible welter of marching armies, of alarums and excursions, and of implausible single combat. Yet the mere fact that so many of Shakespeare's plays end in this way should lead us to the obvious conclusion that these battle-sequences were not only popular but also highly effective in the Elizabethan playhouse. If we study them closely, we find that here, as in every feature of his poetic drama, Shakespeare had a sure sense of what was relevant and dramatically important in his story. In MACBETH, certainly, the design is quite clear. Presented in the conditions for which the play was written, Act V reveals its taut economy and logical shape. Macbeth is strongly fortifying great Dunsinane: he is therefore beleaguered up aloft, in that part of the Tiring-House which has so often served for battlements: he appears only on the upper level, until his final desperate sortie (V.vii). Meanwhile the liberating forces march and countermarch on the Stage below. Reinforcing this geographical arrangement is the continuous imagery of sickness (Macbeth's 'distemper'd cause') and healing (Malcolm being 'the Med'cine of the sickly Weal'). For Macbeth's loud-mouthed bullying (V.iii) is interrupted by the Doctor, emerging from within with his sceptical diagnosis of the Queen's sickness; and again (V.v) the tyrant's defiance is interrupted from the same quarter by the news of the Queen's death.

This pattern is established at the very start of Act V; for the scene of Lady Macbeth's sleep-walking takes place aloft in the Chamber. The idea of acting this famous scene on the upper level will perhaps not recommend itself to the star-actress. But the pattern of Shakespeare's last Act demands it. The Jacobean boy-player had to obey instructions: he could be put (quite literally) in his place. In the Chamber, the tyrant's distempered cause is hemmed in and imprisoned—'cabin'd, cribb'd, confin'd, bound in To saucy doubts, and fears'—while the liberators, bringing a healing purge to their country, march freely on the broad Stage below. Even during this scene while we are chiefly concerned with the personal tragedy of Lady Macbeth, Shakespeare does not allow us to forget the public traffic of his play. An oblique reference of the Gentlewoman's (**Since his Majesty went into the Field . . .**) reinforces the sense of an impending campaign established in the previous scene. And the Doctor's final judgement upon what he has seen and heard focuses the relation between the Lady's sickness of mind and the sickness of the disordered realm:

Foul whisp'rings are abroad: unnatural deeds
Do breed unnatural troubles . . .

In the poet's habitual manner of insistent relevance, the first words of the scene plant us firmly in the circumstances of the new situation: **I have two Nights watch'd with you . . . When was it she last walk'd?** The Doctor, we notice, is at first sceptical: he is inclined to discredit the Gentlewoman's story, which is, even to us, puzzling in its detail (and it seems to be Shakespeare's deliberate intention that we should only guess at the significance of the sleeper's midnight letter-writing). We hear from the Doctor a quizzical sarcasm in such phrases as **A great perturbation in Nature . . .** and **this slumb'ry agitation**. The effect when later he is convinced is the more compelling. The Gentlewoman, a little pompous and bridling at his raillery, is a stickler for propriety, a loyal and obstinate confidante, with a proper pride in the etiquette of her position: she has described her Lady's **walking, and other actual performances** (what she has done); she will not **report after her** what she has been heard to say. Both these characters are vividly sketched: the Doctor indeed is further developed in a later scene.

Enter Lady, with a Taper. The little glimmering light, and the **Night-Gown** which she has thrown upon her, visibly bring the atmosphere of night to the daylit Chamber. John Edmans does not play this scene with the glassy stare and sickly monotone of the somnambulist. He has been instructed to make us see pictures in the mind's eye, to re-create or re-enact several crucial moments of the play's story—some that we have witnessed, and some whose horror we can only guess at. The continuity, the association of ideas, disappears from time to time, as the sick Queen loses the thread of her thoughts: but the recollected moments, in isolation, are stark and vivid enough. She comes in with her taper in her hand, then holds the other hand to the flame, to see if there is still a stain upon it. The concentration of the audience's rapt attention upon the hand reminds us inevitably of that earlier time when the blood-stained hands of Macbeth and his wife were the visible token of the murder of Duncan. Now the commentary of the two watchers interprets for us a detail which in the daylit playhouse we might otherwise have missed:

—You see her eyes are open.
—Ay but their sense are shut.

She puts the taper down on a table and falls to rubbing the place. But it is vain: the stain will not go. **Yet here's a spot.** The Doctor whips out his note-book to record her speech: he **will set down what comes from her**: he is little prepared for what in the event he hears.

One: Two: Why then 'tis time to do't.

It is the little bell, two clinking strokes ('Go bid thy Mistress, when my drink is ready, She strike upon the Bell'). We are back in imagination at the moment of waiting while her husband is about the business of Duncan's murder.

Hell is murky . . .

She finds now what it is to be palled 'in the dunnest smoke of Hell'. That is why **she has light by her continually, 'tis her command.** In her dream she seems briefly to draw confidence from the **power** of sovereignty; but at once it fails her:

> **yet who would have thought the old man to have
> had so much blood in him . . .**

We remember her saying 'Had he not resembled My Father as he slept, I had done't'. We remember 'His Silver skin lac'd with his Golden Blood'. Her husband's ghoulishly extravagant description (of what she had herself seen) had made her faint.

The Thane of Fife, had a wife:

(like a nursery jingle—fie, foh, and fumme)

where is she now?

It was Lady Macduff: 'What, All my pretty Chickens, and their Dam At one fell swoop?'

No more o'that my Lord, no more o'that: you mar all with this starting.

Is this an echo of Banquo's ghostly appearance at the feast? Again she struggles to rub the stain from her hand. The smell haunts her: **all the perfumes of Arabia** would not help.

Oh, oh, oh . . .

Three deep-drawn sighs, each more eloquent than the last: the boy-player does not shrink from giving them full voice. **What a sigh is there!** whispers the Doctor from his corner: **The heart is sorely charg'd**. That is the sort of sound John Edmans makes us hear: the heart charged. Urgently she cries to her husband:

Wash your hands, put on your Night-Gown . . .

We see him again, standing helpless, lost so poorly in his thoughts. We remember her former confidence, so ironically mistaken: 'A little Water clears us of this deed. How easy is it then!' Now her concentration slips again, and we are given a glimpse of a conversation we have not witnessed, but whose tenour is easily guessed:

I tell you yet again Banquo's buried; he cannot come out on's grave.

The Doctor's whispered comment, **Even so?**, registers the fact that for him the name of Banquo reveals a new crime. Then instantly we are back at Duncan's murder:

There's knocking at the gate.

We remember it, out there, outside the Door: 'Here's a knocking indeed: if a man were Porter of Hell Gate . . . Who's there i'th'name of Belzebub?' She is dragging his reluctant hand:

Come, come, come, come . . .

each repetition is more urgent, as we feel his paralysed resistance.

What's done, cannot be undone.

Here is the last statement of a recurrent and dominantly pervasive motif. The word 'done', especially associated in the first part of the play with a conflict of purpose, has come now to express with the full force of iteration the tragedy of irrevocable action and its consequences. The cry is wrung from her sorely charged heart: it is a stage further in despair than the cold comfort of her earlier phrase: 'what's done, is done'. The falling cadence of her last words—

To bed, to bed, to bed . . .

reminds us of another repeated motif, that she lacks 'the season of all Natures, sleep'. She goes back where she came—still, in imagination, at Inverness (not Dunsinane) on the night of Duncan's murder (not on the night when the Doctor and her Gentlewoman are watching her). Once again it must be stressed that Shakespeare's medium is the poetic drama, that the words his actors speak create the drama. The substance of this harrowing scene is only partly the sleep-walking of a woman mortally sick; the other part—the larger and (theatrically) more important part—is the recreated series of crises in the past history of the play. Edmans has acquired in his apprenticeship the skill to evoke these pictures in the mind's eye of his audience.

The impression made upon the Doctor is more remarkable because of his previous scepticism. **More needs she the Divine, than the Physician,** is his opinion; a priest, not a doctor, is wanted in this case. There is something especially moving in his prayer: **God, God forgive us all.** He had it (we may suppose) on the tip of his tongue to say 'God forgive her'. Those who think that there is little evidence of Christian feeling in the canon of Shakespeare's plays, should consider this remarkable expression of the spirit of Christian charity. We are invited by the Doctor's phrase to exclaim: 'There, but for the grace of God, go we.' The blinding selfishness of ambition is part of most people's experience. THE TRAGEDY OF MACBETH is more than a simple tale of retributive justice: it is part of Shakespeare's dramatic plan, during the last movement of the play, to compel the sympathy of the audience for the sinners without diminishing our satisfaction in the triumph of goodness. The Gentlewoman is left alone for a moment after the Doctor's departure: then, steeling herself, she returns to her anxious vigil over her failing mistress. The curtains close on the Chamber of sickness, and hereafter we associate one side of the area behind the Chamber with the sick Queen: mortal sickness will haunt the upper level throughout the last Act of the play.

*   *   *

[V.ii.1–31] As the Chamber-curtains close, the sequel is immediate and startling: *Drum and Colours. Enter Menteth, Cathnes, Angus, Lenox, Soldiers.* As soon as we hear the drum, we realise its significance; the forces of opposition are on the march. This is not, however, the invasion from England for which we have been prepared, but the 'worthy Fellows' of whose revolt Rosse had heard the rumour. The four Scottish Thanes and their token army enter by one of the great Doors on to the Stage: they are on their way to join forces with **the English power**, whose leaders are listed for us, **Malcolm, His Uncle Siward, and the good Macduff**: the meeting is likely to be **near Birnam wood**. We can learn something about Shakespeare's stagecraft, even from this brief and seemingly perfunctory scene. The substance of it lies not so much in the characterisation of the participants (for there is little) nor in their action (which is merely preparatory) but in their projection of a new phase in the story. First we hear of the mood of the invaders, in whom **revenges burn**. Then the absence of Donalbain, mentioned in parenthesis, gives occasion for the introduction to our notice of **Siward's Son**, one of the **many unrough youths** who have volunteered for the expedition so that they may **protest their first of Manhood**. We hear, of **the Tyrant**, that

Great Dunsinane he strongly Fortifies.

The conjunction of Dunsinane with Birnam Wood cannot fail to evoke an echo of the Apparition's prophecy. It is some time since we have seen Macbeth: our expectation of his return is quickened by Caithness's description:

> **Some say he's mad: Others, that lesser hate him,**
> **Do call it valiant Fury . . .**

The idea is further developed in Menteith's diagnosis, a little later in the scene, that Macbeth's 'madness' springs from an inner conflict:

> **. . . all that is within him, does condemn**
> **Itself, for being there.**

Shakespeare weaves still closer the texture of his play with strands of previous imagery: the theme of sickness reappears in Macbeth's **distemper'd cause**; the bloody hand of Duncan's murderer in Angus's words,

> **Now does he feel**
> **His secret Murthers sticking on his hands . . .**

The notion of borrowed robes that do not fit recurs most vividly when we hear that

> **Now does he feel his Title**
> **Hang loose about him, like a Giant's Robe**
> **Upon a dwarfish Thief.**

The scene represents the beginning of revolt: Malcolm's liberation of Scotland from tyranny is presented by Caithness in terms of healing:

> **Meet we the Med'cine of the sickly Weal,**
> **And with him pour we in our Country's purge**
> **Each drop of us.**

And Lenox's cadence, acid as ever, contains the same metaphor in his choice of the word 'Sovereign', used in a double sense:

Or so much as it needs,
To dew the Sovereign Flower, and drown the Weeds.

Malcolm is 'the Sovereign Flower' because he is the true King of Scotland; secondly, Caithness's metaphor is picked up, since 'sovereign', to Shakespeare's audience, is the adjective used of medicines which are especially efficacious (Hotspur's popinjay, we remember, considered that 'the Sovereign'st thing on earth Was Parmaceti, for an inward bruise'). The forces of goodness are on the move, and the crusaders' march is stressed in Shakespeare's text: **Well, march we on ... Make we our March towards Birnam**. Birnam is beyond the Door opposite to their entry. *Exeunt marching*, says the Folio; and the direction is repeated at the beginning and end of Scene iv: *Enter ... Marching* and *Exeunt marching*. The relentless rhythm of tramping feet contributes to the sense of Macbeth's being hunted down and penned within his fastness.

*　　*　　*

[V.iii.1–62]   And inevitably, when the Chamber-curtains reopen, we see the tyrant himself, within great Dunsinane. The continuity of this last Act, reflected in the distribution of scenes in the playhouse, is insistent. Just as the previous scene has prepared us for a view of the beleaguered Macbeth, so the first words of this scene recognise the defection of the Thanes which we have just seen on the Stage below: **let them fly all**. Is the tyrant mad? Or is it valiant fury? The questions are still beating in our minds. Certainly his confidence has a feverish quality: he has not ceased to put his faith in the prophecy of the Apparitions:

Till Birnam wood remove to Dunsinane,
I cannot taint with Fear ...

and we realise (with a quickening of the pulse) that the rebels and the

invaders have a rendezvous at Birnam. The solution of another enigma
has yet to be revealed:

**Fear not, Macbeth, no man that's born of woman
Shall e'er have power upon thee.**

The extravagance of Macbeth's boasting is with startling suddenness
interrupted by the disproportionate violence of his bullying tone, as
he hectors the **cream-fac'd Loon**: both moods are indicative of his
own frayed nerves. Yet a new vein of despairing regret begins to find
expression, as he speaks privately to the audience: the weary phrases
of disillusionment are thrown into sharp relief against a counterpoint of
impatient clamour and restless action: this counterpoint is embodied
in the name (shouted in compelling iteration) and the person of Macbeth's armour-bearer:

**Seyton! I am sick at heart
When I behold—Seyton, I say . . .
I have liv'd long enough: my way of life
Is fall'n into the Sere, the yellow Leaf . . .**

We have heard from Angus in the previous scene that 'Those he
commands, move only in command, Nothing in love': and it is
certainly part of Shakespeare's purpose to win some measure of
sympathy for his protagonist in his decline. The note is clearly sounded
in his sense of isolation and his recognition that he has forfeited the
comforting accompaniments of old age,

As Honour, Love, Obedience, Troops of Friends . . .

At last Seyton responds to his summons. This character is no cipher:
the player's demeanour suggests either pity or contempt (perhaps
both) for his master's loss of self-control. For Macbeth is eager to
fight: but there is no one to fight with yet. Seyton, protesting, at-
tempts more than once to fasten some part of his armour on him:
Macbeth jerks away, issuing vain commands with loud-mouthed

bravado. Suddenly he finds the Doctor at his elbow. Although the Folio direction for the beginning of the scene is *Enter Macbeth, Doctor, and Attendants*, it is not unknown for directions of this kind to anticipate later entries: it seems likely that the Doctor enters at *line 36*, just before Macbeth speaks to him: he has crept forth from the sick-room, that area behind the Chamber where we saw the sleeping Queen retire to bed.

> **How does your Patient, Doctor?**

The diagnosis, that **she is troubled with thick-coming Fancies**, is not to Macbeth's liking:

> **Cure her of that:**
> **Canst thou not Minister to a mind diseas'd,**
> **Pluck from the Memory a rooted Sorrow,**
> **Raze out the written troubles of the Brain . . . ?**

The eloquent phrases recoil upon himself: he too needs **some sweet Oblivious Antidote** to **Cleanse the stuff'd bosom, of that perilous stuff Which weighs upon the heart.** The Doctor's reply, **Therein the Patient Must minister to himself,** contains a thinly veiled reproof. Macbeth's retort is violent, railing upon the Doctor, and shouting again to Seyton for his armour. The touch of scornful humour, the savage jesting, is a characteristic feature of Macbeth's heroic desperation:

> **If thou could'st Doctor, cast**
> **The Water of my Land . . .**
> **What Rhubarb, Senna, or what Purgative drug**
> **Would scour these English hence . . . ?**

The imagery of sickness and healing is again prominent, and the presence of the Doctor and the suggested proximity of his patient give to this theme the scene's principal emphasis: its location in the confining limits of the Chamber reinforces this emphasis, and that sickness of the mind which plagues Lady Macbeth and her husband has come to be identified by analogy with the sickness of Scotland. The Doctor is not easily put down: **hear'st thou of them?** asks Macbeth, and the sarcastic stress (which falls rhythmically upon 'Makes', the first word in the line) is clearly pointed in the reply:

> **Ay my good Lord: your Royal Preparation**
> **Makes us hear something.**

As the tyrant storms off, with a return of his blustering bravado, Seyton hovers in the background, the armour still in his hands, and is a sympathetic listener to the Doctor's final couplet—an outburst of pawky humour, which takes the audience too into smiling confidence: Macbeth has expressed his fearlessness in a seemingly final rhyming couplet:

> **I will not be afraid of Death and Bane,**
> **Till Birnam Forest come to Dunsinane.**

The Doctor's epilogue is also couched in rhyme and has the nature of a parody:

> **Were I from Dunsinane away, and clear,**
> **Profit again should hardly draw me here.**

The patient shrugging squire and the canny professional provide an eloquent if reserved comment on the excesses of their tyrannical employer, whose 'pester'd Senses' (in Menteith's phrase) 'recoil, and start, When all that is within him, does condemn Itself, for being there'.

*　　*　　*

[V.iv.1–22]　Again the *Drum* beats: again the *Soldiers* are *Marching*: and this time there is a contrast of *Colours*, perhaps too of uniforms, as the Stage fills with the token representatives of two armies. The rebellious Thanes and the English liberators have met. We have our first sight of Siward who (if the order of the stage-direction is significant) is at Malcolm's side ('An older, and a better Soldier, none That Christendom gives out'). Moreover, although he has no cause to speak in this scene, the Folio makes plain that *Seywards Sonne* is also conspicuous among the invaders. Siward points straight out over the heads of the groundlings as he asks

What wood is this before us?

and Malcolm stares through the back wall of the auditorium as he gives his explicit instruction for camouflage, so startling in the context: the narrative texture of this last movement is closely woven; the preceding scene both began and ended with Macbeth's confident assertion of the impossibility that Birnam Wood should come to Dunsinane; now the order is given:

Let every Soldier hew him down a Bough,
And bear't before him, thereby shall we shadow
The numbers of our Host...

We hear that the **confident Tyrant Keeps still in Dunsinane**, and intends to stand a siege. Malcolm's buoyant optimism is gently rebuked by Macduff, and Siward too adds the weight of his experience to moderate the young man's impulsiveness. His four-square rhyming couplets give ballast to the enterprise:

Thoughts speculative, their unsure hopes relate,
But certain issue, strokes must arbitrate.

Exeunt marching. The feet of the avenging hunters tramp relentlessly towards their quarry.

*   *   *

[V.v.1–28] It should be recognised that Shakespeare's last Act is one long continuous movement, gathering to a head: it is built of alternating contrasts between the free-ranging liberators on the Stage below, and the beleaguered tyrant, penned in his stronghold above: the architecture of the playhouse gives sharp definition to this alternating design. Macbeth, we have been told, keeps resolutely within Dunsinane, and no sooner have the invading forces left the Stage than we hear the tyrant's *Drum*, different in tone from the previous drumming of his enemies, and see his *Colours*. A spectacular effect is made of this moment; for the defiant order,

Hang out our Banners on the outward walls . . .

is met with an immediate and visible response: his soldiers plant his standards on either edge of the upper level and add a touch of brilliant colour to the Tiring-House which survives until the end of the play:

our Castle's strength
Will laugh a Siege to scorn . . .

and the besiegers are to be left to waste away with hunger and disease. Malcolm has already recognised that this policy of remaining within the Castle is Macbeth's 'main hope'. Burbage is in full cry of alliterative braggadocio when he is interrupted by an uncanny and unexpected outbreak of clamour from beyond the walls of the Chamber: *A Cry within of Women*. Whatever sequence of sounds has been devised and rehearsed by the book-keeper in the Tiring-House to fulfil this direction, it makes our hair stand on end. Seyton runs to investigate; and by a skilful device, typical of the poetic drama, Shakespeare makes use of Macbeth's protestation of invulnerability, of having **almost forgot the taste of Fears**, to shake his audience:

The time has been, my senses would have cool'd
To hear a Night-shriek,

(Methought I heard a voice cry . . .)

and my Fell of hair
Would at a dismal Treatise rouse, and stir
As life were in't.

It is our own present condition that he describes.

Seyton returns. His bare announcement, **The Queen (my Lord) is dead**, is followed by silence, long enough for us to be puzzled by Macbeth's impassive reaction, to wonder what (at this climactic moment) he will say: she was once to him 'my dearest Partner of Greatness'. What he says is not callous: but there is no leisure now to do justice to so great a theme: in just such a way Brutus must postpone the expression of his grief for the death of Cassius: 'Friends I owe mo tears To this dead man, than you shall see me pay. I shall find time, Cassius: I shall find time': so now Macbeth:

She should have di'd hereafter;
There would have been a time for such a word.

Burbage's voice dwells on the word 'There', inverting the iambic stress at the beginning of the line: 'There' means 'in the hereafter', in the rest of his days: and thought of his way of life (fall'n into the Sere), without his partner, draws from him his memorable reflection on the futility of all human life. Once again Burbage dominates the play-house from the centre of the upper level. The famous cadences have become hackneyed, but they were once fire-new from the mint of the poet's brain. Their verbal music is carefully studied by both playwright and player. The iteration of

To-morrow, and to-morrow, and to-morrow . . .

matches the weary monotony of the sense, in which each of these tomorrows is subject of the verb 'creeps'. The triple iambic stress of 'tomorrow' is answered by the trochaic opening of the following line:

Creeps in this petty pace . . .

The dying fall sounded by **the last Syllable of Recorded time** is revived in the equal stresses of **all our yesterdays . . .** Wholly characteristic of Shakespeare's genius is the stroke of inspiration with which he brings this elegiac valediction to a full close. The familiar and favourite metaphor of the playhouse is as apt as it is unexpected: Macbeth, standing centrally on the upper level, compares **Life**—his Lady's life, his own life, everybody's life—to **a walking Shadow, a poor Player**, such a one as Richard Burbage. It is a device that Shakespeare has used before, when Hamlet compared his real grief with the artificial passion of the player. In both cases—for Burbage-Hamlet and Burbage-Macbeth—the illusion of reality is strengthened by the juxtaposition. Here Burbage's thumb-nail sketch of the player

That struts and frets his hour upon the Stage . . .

is capped with the ranting of a lunatic's discordant cry:

It is a Tale
Told by an Idiot, full of sound and fury . . .

but the last two words drop away in whispered bathos—

Signifying nothing.

His wife's death has led Macbeth from a sense of isolation to this final disillusionment. Once again through this insight offered to the audience a tale of simple retribution is raised to the stature of tragedy.

[29–52] The mood of reflection is suddenly interrupted by a breathless and panic-stricken scout (who has been keeping his **watch upon the Hill**). Macbeth's 'valiant Fury' increases with each episode. This unlucky messenger is gripped by the throat and bent backward over the parapet of the upper level: one hand is free to point towards the back of the audience as he describes the relentless advance of Birnam Wood:

Within this three Mile may you see it coming.
I say, a moving Grove.

As Burbage threatens to have him hanged alive on **the next Tree,** the neighbouring Stage-Post before his eyes is an appropriate focus for his gesture. Coming so soon after the news of his partner's death, the messenger's report precipitates the crisis: Macbeth's confidence in his invulnerability is shaken, and his doubt makes him **pull in Resolution**. The fine phrase, **th'Equivocation of the Fiend, That lies like truth**, finer still in Shakespeare's day, with the gusto of its topical allusion to the Jesuit Garnet, sounds again the note of that pervasive theme of truthfulness and deception: but now Macbeth is beginning to understand this fine distinction. Growling doubts merge into a desperate defiance, involving in his own ruin a reckless wish, yet again, for universal destruction:

> **There is nor flying hence, nor tarrying here.**
> **I 'gin to be aweary of the Sun,**
> **And wish th'estate o'th'world were now undone.**

The scene which began *fortissimo* with the beating of Macbeth's drum, ends *fortissimo* with the clatter of the great alarum-bell and the bustle of soldiers rushing to arms:

> **Ring the Alarum Bell: blow Wind, come wrack,**
> **At least we'll die with Harness on our back.**

Next time we see the tyrant, he will have left his beleaguered castle, his 'main hope', and will sally forth on to the Stage itself, prepared to die fighting.

*   *   *

[V.vi.1–10] But before that, the King's Men beguile the eyes of their audience with a spectacular stage-effect:

> *Drumme and Colours.*
> *Enter Malcolme, Seyward, Macduffe, and their Army,*
> *with Boughes.*

The whole Stage fills with branches cut by the hired men from the trees on the Bank-side. For a moment the playhouse looks and feels, even smells, like a forest. Macbeth's messenger saw 'a moving Grove'; and we too, so insistent is the continuity of this last Act, see Birnam Wood come to Dunsinane. Then Malcolm gives his order:

**Now near enough: your leavy Screens throw down,
And show like those you are.**

So the invading forces throw their boughs to the ground (disposing them, no doubt, round the base of the Stage-Posts or against the Tiring-House wall, so that there will be room for the combatants to manoeuvre). The effect thus swiftly and economically made, Shakespeare proceeds to define the pattern for the battle: Siward is to lead the assault, and Malcolm expressly includes in this honourable assignment

. . . my Cousin your right Noble Son.

He himself and Macduff will follow in support. Then without further ado the trumpets sound for the advance: they too (in the manner of the poetic drama) are embodied and characterised in the poet's text:

**Make all our Trumpets speak, give them all breath,
Those clamorous Harbingers of Blood, and Death.**

It seems likely that, while the trumpets are blowing, the leaders take part in a ceremonial embrace. In a parallel situation, in 1 HENRY IV (V.ii.97 ff.), Hotspur gives the order: 'Sound all the lofty Instruments of War, And by that Music, let us all embrace: For heaven to earth, some of us never shall, A second time do such a courtesy'; and in that play the Folio adds the stage-direction: *They embrace, the Trumpets sound . . . alarum unto the battell.* Now, when Malcolm and his allies have left the Stage, the Alarums begin, which to Shakespeare's audience are the conventional sign that battle is in progress. The Folio direction here is *Alarums continued*; perhaps the effect was prolonged to suggest the passage of time, and to cover the opening of the Study-curtains.

*   *   *

[V.vii.1–23] For it is tempting to suppose that at this moment some indication appeared in the Study-space of the Castle wall and gates—a familiar item of furniture in the Study.[18] From these gates we can witness the actual fact of Macbeth's desperate defiance—'Arm, Arm, and out . . . There is nor flying hence, nor tarrying here.' He is in full armour, Bellona's bridegroom, lapped in proof: and his emergence thus at ground level, after being at safe distance aloft for so long, is formidable: we suddenly realise that he is within arm's length. This desperate decision to abandon the strategy, so carefully explained to us, of laughing the siege to scorn from within his impregnable fortification, is thus given visible embodiment in the playhouse. Burbage has the histrionic power to make the groundlings tremble; his metaphor, and his posture, recall to them the familiar scenes of the neighbouring Bear-Garden, where a spectator may tarre on the dogs but would be foolish to come within range himself:

> **They have tied me to a stake, I cannot fly,**
> **But Bear-like I must fight the course.**

Desperate though his situation is, Macbeth is still fearless, trusting in the seemingly infallible promise of the second Apparition:

> **What's he**
> **That was not born of Woman? Such a one**
> **Am I to fear, or none.**

The death of young Siward, carefully prepared for in previous mention and emphasis, is a necessary part of Shakespeare's structure. That he should be killed by Macbeth himself is Shakespeare's invention: he made dramatic capital out of a passing reference in Holinshed: 'It is recorded also, that . . . one of Siwards sonnes chanced to be slaine' (Holinshed goes on to describe the grief and pride of old Siward).

Shakespeare's design is to show that Macbeth appears, to himself and us, invincible: young Siward stirs the heart with his bold challenge to the **abhorred Tyrant,** but, when it comes to sword-play, he is no match for the seasoned warrior's experience. As he falls dead, Macbeth callously exults in his easy conquest, repeating again the grounds of his confidence:

> **Thou wast born of woman;**
> **But Swords I smile at, Weapons laugh to scorn,**
> **Brandish'd by man that's of a Woman born.**

The iteration of the words of the prophecy is the poet's way of preparing us for his climax.

As Macbeth leaves the Stage by one Door, the *Alarums* of battle are renewed in the direction of his departure: he has gone into the thick of the fray. Next moment Macduff enters from the opposite Door, and guesses by the direction of the din (**That way the noise is**) that he is near to catching up with his quarry: he seeks only Macbeth; his one fear is that someone else will rob him of his revenge:

> **If thou beest slain, and with no stroke of mine,**
> **My Wife and Children's Ghosts will haunt me still.**

Again the Alarums break out, and again the sound, and its significance, are embodied in the speaker's words:

> **There thou should'st be,**
> **By this great clatter, one of greatest note**
> **Seems bruited.**

With a prayer on his lips, **Let me find him Fortune,** he plunges into the fray on the heels of his enemy.

[24–29] The action on the Stage is continuous: and though there is no geographical realism in the sequence, the points of emphasis in the narrative are carefully chosen by the dramatist. For the moment the personal fortunes of Macbeth are forgotten and we return to the general direction of the siege. The *Alarums* die down, and our attention is focused upon the gates in the Study, which are now thrown open. Soldiers of the invading army run in and stand each side of the opening: Siward follows, leading Malcolm:

This way my Lord, the Castle's gently rend'red.

Dunsinane has yielded to the attackers. All enter the gates, except perhaps Rosse, who catches sight of young Siward's dead body, hitherto unobserved on the perimeter beyond one of the Stage-Posts. The expression of concern on his face is not unknown to us in past experience, and will prepare us now for the later scene when he reports his discovery of the young man's death in battle to his father. He orders two soldiers to carry him into the Castle, and himself follows last.

[30–63]   And so the Stage is clear for the final confrontation. An *Alarum* renews the context of battle, and Macbeth reappears, still full of fight, refusing to **play the Roman Fool** and take his own life. His intention to plunge once more into the fray is halted by the arresting cry of Macduff, in hot pursuit:

Turn Hell-hound, turn.

We have scarcely time to remark a note of compunction in Macbeth's words, **my soul is too much charg'd With blood of thine already,** when swords are crossed and the duel begins. It is no perfunctory affair, of 'one, two, and the third in your bosom': Burbage is an expert swordsman and, for all his nearly forty years, will not disappoint the groundlings' expectation. A prolonged exchange of parry and thrust (to which *Fight* the Folio adds the accompaniment of an *Alarum*) ends in 'nothing neither way', and the panting combatants draw off. Unruffled, confident, invulnerable, Macbeth tells Macduff that he is wasting his time: **Thou losest labour.** Triumphantly he boasts of his infallible grounds of assurance:

**I bear a charmed Life, which must not yield
To one of woman born.**

His adversary's answer, on first hearing at the Globe, is an astonishing *coup de théâtre*:

> **Despair thy Charm,**
> **And let the Angel whom thou still hast serv'd**
> **Tell thee, Macduff was from his Mother's womb**
> **Untimely ripp'd.**

We in the audience are thunderstruck, but the effect upon Macbeth is no less extraordinary: the great warrior, the brave Macbeth ('well he deserves that Name'), collapses, crumbles, falteringly admits that the news **hath Cow'd my better part of man.** We hear then the last outraged acknowledgement of the Equivocation that lies like truth (Banquo had warned his noble partner long ago that 'the Instruments of Darkness tell us Truths . . . to betray's In deepest consequence'):

> **And be these Juggling Fiends no more believ'd,**
> **That palter with us in a double sense,**
> **That keep the word of promise to our ear,**
> **And break it to our hope. I'll not fight with thee.**

A tame surrender then? To **live to be the show, and gaze o'th'time?** exhibited like **our rarer Monsters,**

> **Painted upon a pole, and under-writ,**
> **Here may you see the Tyrant.**

No doubt, some of the common soldiers have witnessed the duel, afraid at first to say what champion they favour: no doubt, they laugh at Macduff's mocking picture. But Macbeth silences their sneers, with a threatening gesture in their direction: he will not **be baited with the Rabble's curse.** His last defiance is heroic, against all the odds:

> **Though Birnam wood be come to Dunsinane,**
> **And thou oppos'd, being of no woman born,**
> **Yet I will try the last.**

The duel is renewed and Macduff drives him off-stage through one of the great Doors. The *Alarums* begin once more. The soldiers follow into the Doorway and watch the end on tip-toe. At the climax of the din, Macbeth's death-cry is heard over-topping all. Then suddenly there is silence. The Stage is empty.[19]

[64–104] After a pause, a single trumpet blows a falling cadence, instantly recognised in the playhouse as the familiar sounding of the *Retreat*. The battle is lost, and won. Then all the brass bursts forth in a triumphant *Flourish*. The Stage fills rapidly with the victorious troops (*with Drumme and Colours*) flooding in from both Doors. Malcolm, Siward, Rosse and the other Thanes enter through the Castle-gates. Malcolm is in the centre, with Siward at one side of him and Rosse at the other. The ever-gentle Rosse breaks the news of young Siward's death with the tact and dignity we have come to expect of him. The brief scene of the old general's stoicism is given ample space (neither too much nor too little):

> They say he parted well, and paid his score,
> And so God be with him.

It is a welcome interlude of calm (establishing yet again that these are indeed 'God's soldiers') between the noise of battle which precedes it and the gruesome sequel.

Gruesome it is, not laughable—this head which Macduff bears in, raised aloft on his sword's point. It draws gasps of fascinated horror from the soldiers, and 'curses, not loud but deep' from the nobility. Now as the whole company hail Malcolm **King of Scotland**, while the trumpets blow their ceremonial *Flourish*, Macduff lifts his trophy up to Macbeth's revolted soldiers on the upper level, and they fix his head (for all the world like the merciless Macdonwald's) upon our battlements. This position of the head reminds us poignantly of the moment not so long ago when Macbeth from the same place told us that 'all our yesterdays, have lighted Fools The way to dusty death'. Now those lips are closed. It will be hard to keep our attention on Malcolm's glib summing-up—the creation of Scotland's first **Earls**, the mention (almost in parenthesis) of Lady Macbeth's suicide, the plans for his own coronation—while this head lowers at us from aloft. **This dead Butcher** is Malcolm's characteristic simplification, but while a final *Flourish* of trumpets carries the actors off the Stage, proclaiming that Scotland sees her wholesome days again, we in the audience must be thinking: This was Bellona's bridegroom, valour's minion, who once bought golden opinions from all sorts of people. This was he who gave his eternal jewel to the common enemy of man, and who learnt too late that what's done cannot be undone. Wake Duncan with thy knocking. I would thou could'st.

NOTES

Page 23

1 John P. Cutts, *Musique de la Troupe de Shakespeare*, prints a contemporary setting of one of the songs (*Come away, come away*), and the music for two Witches' Dances, all by Robert Johnson. Cutts argues that one of the dances figured in Ben Jonson's *Masque of Queenes* (1609), became very popular and subsequently found its way, via *The Witch*, to MACBETH; the other was apparently written as a pendant to the first, specially for MACBETH. There is additional support for the theory that the Hecate scenes are a later interpolation, in Bernard Beckerman's argument (*Shakespeare at the Globe*, 93 f.) that the King's Men did not make use of flying machinery until they began to perform at the Blackfriars, and that 'for the Globe, at least so far as the plays demonstrate, no machinery for flying existed'. At the end of Hecate's first speech there is a strong hint that she ascends to the Heavens in 'a Foggy cloud'.

Page 41

2 In 1603 Samuel Harsnet, secretary to Bishop Bancroft (later Archbishop of Canterbury), published his *Declaration of Egregious Popish Impostures*, which denounced witchcraft as fraudulent and often the result of Catholic machinations. This book enjoyed much popularity after the Gunpowder Plot, when public feeling was inflamed against the Jesuits, and many references in KING LEAR show that Shakespeare had read it.

Page 44

3 In his account of MACBETH at the Globe, Forman relates that Macbeth and Banquo were 'Riding thorowe a wod' when there stood before them '3 women feiries or Nimphes'. There seems no reason to deduce from this description that there were trees on the stage to represent a wood, or that the players made 'skilled use of hobby-horses' (Nevill Coghill, *Shakespeare's Professional Skills*, 206). There are several unlikely details in Forman's account—he claims, for instance, that at some point in the performance Duncan made Macbeth

'Prince of Northumberland'. Moreover the fact that Forman calls the Witches 'feiries or Nimphes' (descriptive terms wholly unsuitable to Shakespeare's Witches) strongly suggests that he had read Holinshed's narrative, and that it had become confused in his memory with Shakespeare's play. His description of the meeting with the Witches seems to reflect the well-known illustration in Holinshed; it may even be a recollection of the relevant passage, since Holinshed tells us that Macbeth and Banquo passed 'thorough the woods and fields' on their way to Forres.

Page 47

4 T. J. King, *Shakespearean Staging, 1599–1642*, 84 f., argues that 'a trap to the place below was probably used for staging scenes in which actors *vanish*. *Macbeth* has *Witches vanish* followed by Banquo's line "The Earth hath bubbles, as the Water ha's . . ." which strongly implies that the actors drop through a trap.' This arrangement is certainly possible for the Witches' departure; but there is something clumsy about the congestion of all three players vanishing through the trap. The bubbling earth is complemented by a melting 'into the Air . . . as breath into the Wind'. Yet we are surely not to deduce from this that one of the trio was hoisted up to the Heavens on a wire.

Page 48

5 The idea that Macbeth's honours are 'borrowed Robes' which do not fit him recurs several times in the play; it is implied in Banquo's lines I.iii.144 ff.; Caithness hints at it in V.ii.15 f.; Angus states it more explicitly in V.ii.20 ff.; Lady Macbeth's taunt in I.vii.35 f. echoes it ironically. In II.iv.38 Macduff applies the same image to Macbeth's subjects.

Page 56

6 The word 'kind', apart from bearing its usual sense of 'benevolent', was also used by the Elizabethans, more fundamentally, to mean 'natural'; hence 'kindness' could mean either 'benevolence' or 'nature', or both. Thus the phrase 'too full o'th'Milk of human kindness' may indicate merely that Macbeth is too sentimentally benevolent; it may also mean that he is reluctant to deny his nature as a human being by committing an unnatural deed (Moulton suggested that the phrase should be written 'humankind-ness' to make this second connotation clear). It is likely that the phrase bears both meanings at once, and we may paraphrase thus: 'Macbeth is too full of the benevolence, or sentimentality, which is part of the true nature of every human being.'

Page 60

7 We assume the accepted interpretation of these lines. But it must be observed that the Folio punctuation suggests a different interpretation, which, although less successful dramatically, at least makes acceptable sense:

> Your Face, my *Thane*, is as a Booke, where men
> May reade strange matters, to beguile the time.
> Looke like the time . . .

This may be paraphrased thus: 'Your face is too revealing, like a book where we read of wonders to while away the time.' And then a new idea: 'Assume the same expressions as everybody else.' (For this use of 'beguile the time' cf. TWELFTH NIGHT, III.iii.41 f.: 'Whiles you beguile the time . . . With viewing of the Town.') It is characteristic of Shakespeare to pick up a single word, 'time', and use it immediately in a different sense; cf. HAMLET, I.v.164 f., where to Horatio's exclamation 'Oh day and night: but this is wondrous strange', Hamlet replies 'And therefore as a stranger give it welcome.'

Page 63

8 See *Shakespeare Survey*, vol 12, 47 ff., for a suggestion by Allardyce Nicoll that the direction 'over the Stage' indicated that the actors were to enter through the Yard and ascend on to the Stage from below. King, 147, argues that 'this direction is found in many plays performed at Court where there was no yard, and at other places where perhaps there was no platform stage'.

Page 80

9 It has often been observed that in the phrase 'making the Green one Red' the word 'one' is an adjective qualifying the noun 'red' (in spite of an inconvenient comma placed after it in the Folio): all the green of the multitudinous seas will become one pervading red. It should be added that when the word is given this adjectival sense the short line is less short than it seems; each of the last three monosyllables has the same solemn strength. To avoid a syntactical confusion, we have adopted the usual modern punctuation.

Page 87

10 Editors have long disputed whether Lady Macbeth's fainting-fit is intended to be real, or feigned to create a diversion; the question, fully discussed by Bradley, 484 ff., in terms of real life, can only be answered in the theatre in relation to Lady Macbeth's role in the rest of the play. On the deep Stage of the Globe, it is possible, though not easy, for the player to suggest that the 'faint' is deliberate, but whether or not Lady Macbeth's motive for such diversionary tactics can be made clear is another matter; and Shakespeare has not chosen, as he could have done, to clarify the motive in the dialogue. We have preferred to treat the faint as 'real', another sign of the weakness she has deliberately stifled. Macbeth's description of the murdered King has been lurid enough, and the picture of Duncan lying in his blood haunts her even in her sleep (V.i.42 ff.).

Page 93

11 The reference to Caesar comes as a surprise, until we remember that Shakespeare, busy already in planning his next play, has his Plutarch open on his table. He gave this anecdote of Antony's 'Genius' dramatic form in ANTONY AND CLEOPATRA, II.iii.10 ff. It is interesting that Macbeth, later, rejects the possibility of suicide with the words 'Why should I play the Roman Fool, and die On mine own sword?' Cleopatra, by contrast, speaks of death by suicide as being 'after the high Roman fashion'.

Page 94

12 Most editors take these lines to mean that Macbeth is rebelling against the decrees of Fate; but, if this is the right interpretation, 'champion me' here means 'fight against me', a rather unusual sense. If however 'Fate' here bears its old sense of 'destruction, ruin' (O.E.D.), a less strained interpretation is possible: Macbeth calls upon Destruction to fight *for* him to the utterance, to the bitter end. He again proclaims himself willing to see universal destruction in III.ii.16, IV.i.58 ff., and V.v.49 ff.

13 For similar scenes of temptation, using some of the same persuasive weapons, cf. KING JOHN, III.iii.19 ff., HAMLET, IV.vii.57 ff., THE TEMPEST, II.i. 212 ff. Less subtle is the procedure in RICHARD III (I.iii.339 ff.), where in contrast there is no question of temptation: the *two murtherers* are carefully identified for us by Gloster himself in a helpful aside: 'But soft, here come my Executioners.'

Page 118

14 In the *De Origine, Moribus, et Rebus Gestis Scotorum* of John Leslie, Bishop of Ross, there is a striking illustration of the family tree of the Stuarts. It is labelled 'The genealogy of the royal family of Stuart, which inherits by legitimate succession the throne of Scotland through the unbroken line of eight previous monarchs', and it takes the form of a tree with the name of Banquo at its root; among the branches and about the twisting trunk are circles bearing the names of Banquo's descendants, the direct line of monarchs of which James I was so proud. The illustration is reproduced in *Shakespeare's England*, vol. 2, 536.

Page 120

15 The eight kings represent the Stuarts, from Robert II to Mary, who ruled over Scotland only; when Macbeth peers into the glass he sees a line of kings who carry two-fold orbs, indicating that they rule over both England and Scotland. This union of crowns was brought about by James I's accession to the English throne in 1603. Chambers suggests that the 'treble Sceptres' represent the two sceptres used in the English coronation, and the one used in the Scottish coronation; but they may symbolise the three kingdoms of England, Scotland and Ireland, over which James I ruled.

Page 127

16 We adopt Theobald's widely accepted emendation, 'deserve', of the Folio's 'discerne'. The Folio reading is not impossible.

Page 129

17 According to Holinshed, Malcolm accuses himself of three vices, lechery, avarice and untruthfulness; it is interesting that, although Shakespeare's Malcolm elaborately repudiates the third of these vices (*lines* 128 ff.), he never accuses himself of it; instead he accuses himself of an aggressive spirit and a desire to 'confound all unity'. In thus departing from Holinshed, Shakespeare was paying particular attention to the interests of James I: James wished above all to be considered a 'King of peace', and welcomed the title of *Pacificus*. His 'vision of imposing peace and concord on a continental scale' is examined in detail by D. H. Willson, *King James VI & I*, 271 ff.

Page 153

18 We may infer the use of gates from a comparison of scenes from both early and late plays in the canon; such as 3 Henry VI, V.i, in which Warwick and the Mayor of Coventry on the Walls of the city are invited by the Yorkists to 'ope the City Gates', and three successive armies march through the gates, while the impulsive Richard of Gloster cries 'The Gates are open, let us enter too'; and CORIOLANUS, I.iv.42, where the Folio stage-direction reads *Another Alarum, and Martius followes them to gates, and is shut in.*

Page 157

19 The Folio's directions for Macbeth's death are confusing: *Exeunt fighting. Alarum.* Then, on a new line, *Enter Fighting, and Macbeth slaine.* If the second of these directions is an addition, then it may be an arrangement devised by the actors at some date between the first performances and 1623, to gratify the taste of the sensationalists. There is no exit directed for Macduff, and no possible provision made for the removal of Macbeth's decapitated body. Most editors have jibbed at the re-entry of the combatants. Macduff's later entry with the severed head (an essential feature of Shakespeare's dénouement) is more effective if the duel ends off-stage. But the arrangement suggested by the Folio stage-direction is manifestly not impossible.